Prayers for Pax-Aroo

Prayers for Pax-Aroo
Copyright 2016 Steve Riggs
All Rights Reserved

No part of this work may be reproduced or transmitted in any form or by any means, electronic or mechanical, photocopying, recording, or by any information retrieval or storage system without the express written permission of the author except in the case of short excerpts used in critical review.

ISBN: 978-1-5407-5087-7

Photos courtesy of: Gay Waldman of Waldman Photos

Printed in the United States of America

With love to:

Paxton, my determined little man

With thanks to:

My prayer warriors
My family and friends
Phoenix Children's Hospital
Scottsdale EMS first responders

LIFE IS WHAT HAPPENS TO YOU WHEN
YOU'RE BUSY MAKING OTHER PLANS

Outside Paxton's room, there is a poster on the outside of his door. It announces to those who stand at the door what they should know about the boy inside before they enter.

"Before entering this room you should know
it holds a special boy.
He is silly, he is happy, he is STRONG! He
is Blessed and he is LOVED! He is lifted
in prayer. Although he may be small, He is
MIGHTY!"

PREFACE

Due to the severity of Paxton's condition, only family members and a few friends are allowed into Paxton's room. Other family members and friends wait for the daily postings on Facebook. They rely on these postings for updates on Paxton's condition. At times, a photo is attached to the posting so that those who are not within Paxton's room can see him.

Only those present in Paxton's room at the hospital are able to take in the whole environment in which Paxton lays. Only they can see, hear and feel what is happening within the walls of Paxton's room.

Within Paxton's room, soft and soothing music can be heard. A friend has offered a small radio so that Paxton's room has the gentle sound of music.

Within Paxton's room, a prayer blanket is laid upon Paxton. A group of women have knitted the prayer shawl together while praying for Paxton. These women do not know Paxton but have heard of his accident and offer to create the prayer shawl for him.

Within Paxton's room, there is the constant activity of doctors and nurses monitoring him, conferring to determine the best medical procedures to administer, and answering questions from concerned family members and friends.

Within Paxton's room, there is the quiet sound of voices. Family and friends converse with each other and support each other. There are hugs and tears among these people in the room. All of them hoping for the complete recovery of Paxton and all of them in pain for what they are observing.

Within Paxton's room, family and friends eat food and drink beverages that have been delivered to those within Paxton's room. Some of the people who have brought the food and beverages do not enter Paxton's room. They do not want to intrude but feel compelled to help in any way they can.

Within Paxton's room, the sound of singing and the reading of children's books can be heard. Paxton's favorite songs are sung. His favorite books have been brought from home. And, the hospital has given Paxton more books to be read.

Within Paxton's room, there are stuffed animals upon his bed which have been given to him by the hospital, family and friends. And, there are posters and pictures on the wall which have been colored by some who love him.

Within Paxton's room, family members are talking to Paxton softly while they hold his hands and feet, and kiss him on the forehead. They say "I love you, Paxton", "You are a good boy, Paxton", "We are here for you, Paxton", "You are doing a great job, Paxton", "You are our super hero, Paxton".

Steve Riggs
July 5 • Phoenix, AZ •
In case you hadn't heard our little boy, Paxton, suffered a tragic accident last night. I am not usually one to ask for prayers, but he needs them as he fights for his life. So PLEASE send our baby boy your prayers!!! Please!
Like • Comment • Share • 1515 • 12 shares • Comments

Steve T.: Prayers have been sent! Praying for ya PAX!!
Like • Reply • July 5 at 4:41pm

Alisha G.: We haven't stopped praying 🙏...sending as many prayers and as much love as that little guy can take...hang in there...
Like • Reply • July 5 at 4:45pm

Josh W.: Praying for you guys.
Like • Reply • July 5 at 4:53pm

Desiree M.: Oh my goodness! You have prayers from Shon and I we love you guys!!
Like • Reply • July 5 at 4:55pm

Shanti W.: He has been in my thoughts and prayers since we heard the news last night. Sending you all much love!
Like • Reply • July 5 at 4:59pm

Joshua D.: Sending prayers and love your way brother!
Like • Reply • July 5 at 5:03pm

Nancy B.: Steve, so so sorry for what Pax and all of you are going through. Of course we are all praying for him and you.
Like • Reply • July 5 at 5:10pm

Rob S.: Not sure what happened, but def praying for him and y'all. If you need ANYTHING hit me up bro!
Like • Reply • July 5 at 5:14pm

Shannon S.: If you guys need anything let me know. ♥♥♥
Like • Reply • July 5 at 5:16pm

Erica K.: Prayers sent your way!!
Like • Reply • July 5 at 5:17pm

Rhonda K.: Praying for healing for Paxton.
Like • Reply • July 5 at 5:21pm

Linda G.: him and your family in prayers!! praying for improvement!!
Like • Reply • July 5 at 5:23pm

Jeffrey W.: You are all in our thoughts and prayers
Like • Reply • July 5 at 5:25pm

Anne M.: Many prayers.
Like • Reply • July 5 at 5:32pm

Amy H.: I keep praying so hard, love you all!
Like • Reply • July 5 at 5:39pm

Liz G.: Steve, Mike and I are sending all of our love, thoughts, prayers and everything else we can think of. If there is ANYTHING you need please let us know. Praying Praying Praying ☺🙏📖♥
Like • Reply • July 5 at 5:46pm

Jessica G.: Praying with all my might!
Like • Reply • July 5 at 5:48pm

Shon P.: We are praying for your family, with all of our might!
Like • Reply • July 5 at 5:58pm

Brian W.: Steve, hoping and praying for all of you!
Like • Reply • July 5 at 5:59pm

Brian W.: Hoping and praying for little Pax and all your family...
Like • Reply • July 5 at 6:00pm

Joan T.: I am praying for Pax and all of you as hard as I can, hold on to your hope
Like • Reply • 1 • July 5 at 6:07pm

Diane M.: Have been praying at different times all day and will continue to do so. God is faithful!
Like • Reply • July 5 at 6:07pm

Kathy K.: Tears and prayers to your family, you know we will help however we can. Love you, my hugs might be digital but they are real. I am so wrecked I can't even imagine. I'm sooo sorry. Prayers are nonstop.
Like • Reply • July 5 at 6:17pm

Nicole P.: I love you all! Sending many prayers and lots of love to Pax and the family!
Like • Reply • July 5 at 6:19pm

Shelly S.: We are praying Steve! Love you guys and am soooo sorry to hear about Paxton! ☹🙏 †
Like • Reply • July 5 at 6:23pm

Adam Elizabeth G.: Praying for little Paxton and sending our love brother!
Like • Reply • July 5 at 6:27pm

Rach S.: Praying. I am so sorry you guys are going through this. Please let us know if we can do anything. I don't care what it is. Even if you need a babysitter for the girls. Love your family
Like • Reply • July 5 at 6:56pm

Mike S.: Thoughts and prayers to him and your family.
Like • Reply • July 5 at 7:08pm

Brad J.: You're all in my thoughts, donation sent. Let me know if there's anything else I can do. Like • Reply • 1 • July 5 at 7:49pm

Shannon D.: Please let us know if you guys need anything at all... Sending love and prayers to your sweet boy and whole family!
Like • Reply • July 5 at 7:49pm

Paige H.: So sorry! Praying for you guys. Please let us know if you guys need any help with anything. Thinking of you guys at this time❤
Like • Reply • July 5 at 8:00pm

Amber A.: Praying for you all last night, today and until we hear he's better.
Like • Reply • July 5 at 8:10pm

Lisa M.: So sad and sorry to hear this. I will pray for Paxton and the rest of you as well. Hugs to all of you!
Like • Reply • July 5 at 8:20pm

Brigett L.: So many prayers, love and healing energy to sweet little Paxton!! And big hugs and lots of love to your family Steve!! I am so sorry and we are with you guys even from afar! ❤❤❤
Like • Reply • July 5 at 9:01pm

Mike Meg K.: Praying and hoping for the best.
Like • Reply • July 5 at 9:55pm

Justin F.: Prayers to you and your family buddy!
Like • Reply • July 5 at 10:18pm

Braidon F.: Praying for your son and family
Like • Reply • July 5 at 10:54pm

Tara G.: 🙏🙏🙏...please lean on us if y'all need anything Steve and Deserae! XO
Like • Reply • July 6 at 12:09am

Dedeuc D.: Done!
Like • Reply • July 6 at 11:14am

Meagan S.: Sending love and healing thoughts to you and your family, Steve.
Like • Reply • July 6 at 4:51pm

Steve Riggs
July 6 • Phoenix, AZ •
Thank you all for the out pouring of love and support for Paxton. These last 2 days have been the most difficult of our entire lives. But with the power of prayer and your love and support it helps give us faith, love, and hope. These next few days or even weeks will be crucial in determining whether he makes it. And if so, if and how much brain damage has occurred. So I ask for your prayers again. That if you have a second in your day to stop and pray for his life and a miracle of full recovery. Dez and I thank you from the bottom of our hearts for everything. You never know how much love and support is out there until something like this happens. ❤
Like • Comment • Share • 38 Kim P. and 37 others 2 shares •
Comments

Katie R.: I love you Steve and Dez. Praying so hard for sweet Pax and holding you all close to my heart. ❤❤❤
Like • Reply • July 6 at 6:29am

Sean T.: Constant prayers going out man.
Like • Reply • July 6 at 6:32am

Rhonda K.: Continuing to pray for complete healing for Pax.
Like • Reply • July 6 at 6:37am

Rob S.: Love you guys man. Continuing to pray for y'all, but especially for Pax!
Like • Reply • July 6 at 6:50am

Shannon J.: Thinking about you all day everyday
Like • Reply • July 6 at 6:53am

Anne M.: Praying.
Like • Reply • July 6 at 7:15am

Shelly S.: Loving you guys and prayers continue ....🙏😇 †
Like • Reply • July 6 at 7:17am

Brian W.: Thank you Steve and Dez for the update. Keeping you all in our hearts.
Like • Reply • July 6 at 7:18am

Anissa C.: Love you my extended family I'm praying for you all.
Like • Reply • July 6 at 7:39am

Desiree M.: Constantly praying for your precious baby!
Like • Reply • July 6 at 7:42am

Cassie M.: Praying for sweet Pax and for your strength 🙏🙏🙏 the power of prayer is strong 💜💜💜 please let us know if you guys need anything at all
Like • Reply • July 6 at 8:29am

Rach S.: Love you guys and praying praying praying.
Like • Reply • July 6 at 8:48am

Judy H.: Hang in there, Steve. We love you and are praying for your precious family.
Like • Reply • July 6 at 9:59am

Justin F.: Much love and many prayers for your family and boy!
Like • Reply • July 6 at 10:18am

Myra A.-R.: Sending you guys lots of love 💚 and prayers 🙏
Like • Reply • July 6 at 9:47pm • Edited

Lisa M.: Love and Prayers!
Like • Reply • July 6 at 3:12pm

Liz G.: We love you guys and are praying!!!!
Like • Reply • July 6 at 4:07pm

Meagan S.: Sending so much love and positive thoughts your way, Steve.

Like • Reply • 1 • July 6 at 4:52pm

Fred A.: Our thoughts are with your family
Like • Reply • 1 • July 6 at 9:44pm

Julie R.: Just reading this for the first time... yikes! Catching up -- but nothing but love and prayers!!!!
Like • Reply • July 7 at 9:00pm

Steve Riggs
July 6 •

With the power of love and prayer anything is possible. Brooklyn and Braelyn sing Paxton his favorite song at the hospital. ❤ And 👼

Like • Comment • Share • 44 Katie R., Kim P. and 42 others 15 shares •Comments

Robt W.: Wow.
Like • Reply • July 6 at 2:49pm

Cassie M.: There's so much love surrounding him 👼🔲❤👼🔲❤

Like • Reply • July 6 at 2:52pm

Nicole P.: That's absolutely beautiful!! 🖤🖤🐾
Like • Reply • 1 • July 6 at 3:11pm

Richie Nikki R.: Praying for baby Paxton
Like • Reply • July 6 at 3:12pm

Lisa M.: Hugs to all of you! 💖
Like • Reply • July 6 at 3:14pm

Shelly S.: Hugs, prayers and love to you all!! 🙏💕 †
Like • Reply • July 6 at 3:19pm

Amy H.: So beautiful, good job girls! Keep fighting Pax! Love you all <3
Like • Reply • July 6 at 3:26pm

Shanti W.: <3
Like • Reply • July 6 at 3:33pm

Joan T.: Absolutely beautiful girls, I have no doubt your baby brother heard your song and it made him very happy. 😊
Like • Reply • July 6 at 3:33pm

Rach S.: Wow that made me cry. Thanks for sharing. This is great for Paxton. Hugs
Like • Reply • 1 • July 6 at 3:44pm

Alisha G.: Amazing. A lot of strength in those little girls...we are still praying every day!! 🙏
Like • Reply • 1 • July 6 at 3:51pm

Rob S.: Such a great sight. Got the update from Kaylee too, God is great! Gonna continue praying for little man!
Like • Reply • July 6 at 4:01pm

Adam Elizabeth G.: Both of us are crying, what love and support baby Paxton has. Such amazing big sister's to look over him.
Like • Reply • July 6 at 4:17pm

Jessica G.: Beautiful!!!! I bet he loved it!!!
Like • Reply • July 6 at 6:56pm

Paige H.: This is the sweetest thing ever! I literally cried today as Shay and I were talking about you guys and your baby boy today. We are thinking about you guys and hope things are on the uphill. Are here for you guys at anytime ❤ our prayers and love sent your way!
Like • Reply • 1 • July 7 at 9:30pm

Steve Riggs
July 6 • Phoenix, AZ •
I'm always cautious to post good news. Things are ever changing and we have had moments of hope followed by some scary moments as well... BUT Paxton made some very significant strides today. Strides that even amazed doctors and nurses. He is able to completely sustain a heartbeat on his own. And just now they have turned his ventilator to "auto mode" and he is able to breathe on his own. NOW, we are not nearly out of the woods. At any point his body may decide it's fatigued and he will have to have his ventilator turned back on. But it's a good sign. We also still have to establish the extent of his brain damage that occurred due to swelling and lack of oxygen for so long. But the fact that he is sustaining life on his own is a very positive sign. He also made a couple other strides today that I will hold off on commenting about until the doctors are able to access him better. But in 48 hours he was essentially found dead, admitted in severely critical condition, deemed to be best case scenario severe brain damage, to now sustaining most vital functions on his own (he's obviously not eating due to sedation). So I'll be grateful for what we have and hopeful for a miracle of a recovery. I have honestly felt in my heart the power of prayer. And I have been moved by all the support and love. We are nowhere near out of the woods. So please keep them going. Your prayers are helping every second.
Like • Comment • Share • 46 Katie R., Amber A. and 44 others 1 share • Comments

Meagan S.: Sending love and keeping you all in my heart.
Like • Reply • July 6 at 9:52pm

Brian W.: Thank you Steve, the collective positive will of the people who know you, and those who now know you through this event is strong, powerful, and growing. Take from it all you need, you'll never deplete it! Promise!
Like • Reply • July 6 at 9:53pm

Steve T.: Amazing news and many more prayers coming

Like • Reply • July 6 at 9:56pm

Rob S.: Thanks for the update bro. Continuing to pray for Pax. Love you guys, stay strong!
Like • Reply • 1 • July 6 at 10:01pm

Linda G.: thanks much for updates and praying for Pax and all your family always!! ❤ remember he's strong like you!
Like • Reply • July 6 at 10:06pm • Edited

Jenna S.: He did such a good job today!
Like • Reply • July 6 at 10:16pm

Alisha G.: So grateful to hear this news! We will continue our daily prayers. And keep you and Dez in our hearts...hang in there. Love knows no boundaries....🤗
Like • Reply • July 6 at 10:17pm

Desiree M.: I can't stop thinking of you guys and praying for pax! So glad to hear this positive progress! Sending lots of love to you all 💜
Like • Reply • July 6 at 10:26pm

Amy H.: I love reading such wonderful news. He is such a strong little fighter! You all are in my heart!
Like • Reply • July 6 at 10:42pm

Josh W.: We are praying for your whole family.
Like • Reply • July 6 at 10:45pm

Lisa M.: Power of prayer ☺ ☐ I loved reading this too! Hugs to all of you!
Like • Reply • 1 • July 6 at 10:49pm

Joan T.: These are all huge accomplishments, and I'm so happy to hear them all. Will continue to pray for your sweet baby boy that he continues to improve. Hugs and love to you all!
Like • Reply • July 7 at 4:15am

Kerri C.: GOD is good, he made pax a fighter, small but mighty. Love you guys!!!!!!
Like • Reply • July 7 at 7:28am

Rach S.: Wow love this.... God is working in such powerful ways all around. Thanks for keeping us updated. Hugs
Like   Reply • July 7 at 8:58am

Steve Riggs
July 7 • Phoenix, AZ •
It's never too early for a mother's loving touch.
Like • Comment • Share • 59 Loretta K., Kim P. and 56 others •
Comments

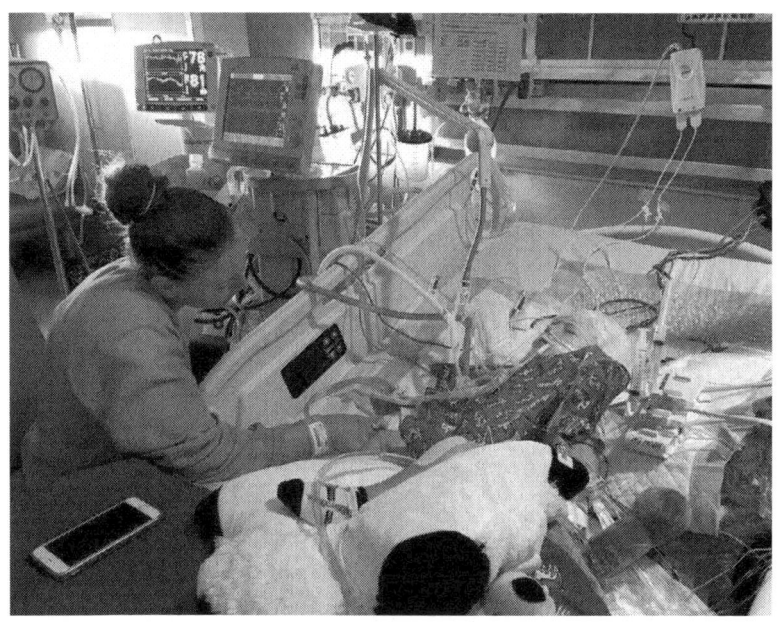

Nancy B.: Thank you so much for posting Steve, we are all so worried about Little Paxton. So happy to hear the positive report - continued love and prayers to you and your family - stay strong Steve, your family is very lucky to have you as their strength. Sending hugs to all of you.
Like • Reply • July 7 at 7:58am

Steele R.: Absolutely, all that love helps the healing process....
What a precious pic.
Like • Reply • July 7 at 9:27am

Etta M.: Steve we did not know about little Paxton. Happy to hear the positive news. Prayers going up.
Like • Reply • July 7 at 11:23am

Liz G.: praying, praying...
Like • Reply • July 8 at 9:09am

Steve Riggs
July 7 • Phoenix, AZ •
Well today was filled with ups and downs. And I am fatigued to the point I'm not sure how clearly my thoughts will be. But the support from you all has been so overwhelming I want you guys to at least be able to be involved with his updates. Today Pax made some good progress. He was able to be taken off some of his sedation medication to test his brain activity. And although there is no clear indication to the extent of the damage, there have been some positive signs. Unfortunately with the good, there also is a little disappointment when there are signs of potential or even probable damage as well. BUT, he is alive and for that we are eternally grateful. He did need to receive a transfusion today due to a sharp decline in his blood cells. And he also battled a fever and problems with the ventilator tube becoming plugged with secretions causing his breathing to stop (SCARY). But on the positive side, he appears to be initiating his own breathing again, his blood count is back up, and his fever is under control. Anyway, what an up and down emotional day. We are all exhausted as is Paxton I'm sure. Tomorrow is a HUGE day for us. They have decided to move up the MRI to tomorrow, which will give us our first visual glimpse internally into Paxton's brain to assess long term damage. So please keep him in your prayers. Thank you all. And I mean that from the bottom of my heart.
Like • Comment • Share • 39 Loretta K., Kim P. and 36 others •
Comments

Rob S.: Love you guys. What time is his MRI? Text us and let us know, want to make sure we are praying during it.
Like • Reply • July 7 at 10:17pm

Desiree M.: Haven't stopped praying for you! I wish I could give you a hug right now Steve!
Like • Reply • July 7 at 10:20pm

Shannon D.: Thank you for the updates! As I said to Dez today, if it's in 3 hours, 3 days or 3 weeks we're here to help...just text us! Food, coffee, hugs or to just be there 🫂
Like • Reply • 1 • July 7 at 10:26pm

Brigett L.: In my mind and prayers all the time!! What a strong little fighter you have! Love to you all!!❤️🖤
Like • Reply • July 7 at 10:31pm

Adam Elizabeth G.: Still praying around the clock, love you guys!
Like • Reply • July 7 at 10:32pm

Brad J.: You are all always on my mind. Wishing you the very best.
Like • Reply • 1 • July 7 at 10:35pm

Jessica G.: Consistently praying for you guys. I know how rough the ups and downs are. But he's a fighter and will get through this
Like • Reply • July 7 at 10:35pm

Amber A.: Praying and thinking of all of you constantly.
Like • Reply • July 7 at 10:38pm

Linda G.: Pax and your family are in my prayers and heart always ❤️
Like • Reply • July 7 at 10:45pm

Justin F.: Much love to you and your family!
Like • Reply • July 7 at 10:47pm

Natalie B.: Praying for you 🙏📖 💚💝
Like • Reply • July 7 at 10:47pm

Julie R.: Hang in there, Steve and Dez -- we are all praying for Pax and your entire family. God Bless!!!!
Like • Reply • July 7 at 10:54pm

Nancy B.: Sending you love and prayers always.
Like • Reply • July 7 at 10:54pm

Myra A.-R.: We are Continuing to pray for him and your family 🙏 I have shared your story to friends and family so that more prayers can come your way. ❤ Surrounding Paxton with the healing light of Christ.
Like • Reply • July 7 at 11:37pm

Jami G.: Praying for your family 🙏
Like • Reply • July 8 at 7:30am

Alisha G.: Will be thinking about you all today...sending love and more prayers!!
Like • Reply • July 8 at 7:56am

Liz G.: Thank you Steve for the updates. I can only imagine how difficult this all is. Please know that Mike and I are waiting for updates from you guys and Paxton is at the forefront of our minds. We have everyone over here praying for his recovery and your family. We love you guys so very much!
Like • Reply • July 8 at 9:15am

Steve Riggs
July 8 • Phoenix, AZ •
Thank you all for your prayers and your strength. Today will be an emotional day for us all. The MRI has been moved up to NOW. Obviously there is no danger with the MRI. But finding out the extent of brain damage is scary. After the MRI they plan to extubate Paxton. And at that point they will take him off of sedation. They will keep him on a feeding tube and his IVs in for meds and such. But we will be able to hold him❤ Whether or not he is able to recognize us is unknown. Well.... Basically all brain function is unknown at this point other than his ability to sustain life. He will be kept here at the hospital of course and physical, speech/occupational therapy will be implemented. As much as I fear the results of the MRI my faith has me confident in recovery. That with the help of God, determined parents and a strong willed little boy we will eventually thrive!! Please keep praying. Thank you everyone who has supported us. Paxton thanks you as well.
Like • Comment • Share • 33 Judy H., Diane M. and 31 others 1 share •Comments

Shannon J.: Love you guys. Hoping for the best today! ❤❤❤
Like • Reply • July 8 at 9:42am

Mike S.: Praying for you all.
Like • Reply • July 8 at 9:52am

Katie R.: Lots of love Steve and Dez.....❤❤❤❤❤❤
Like • Reply • July 8 at 10:00am

Lisa M.: Hugs and prayers!! 💖
Like • Reply • July 8 at 10:06am

Mike Meg K.: Best of luck today!!!
Like • Reply • July 8 at 10:11am

Steve T.: Prayers for you guys and little strong PAXTON!!
Like • Reply • July 8 at 10:11am

Desiree M.: Prayers and love to you all!
Like • Reply • July 8 at 10:31am

Nancy B.: Love 🖤 and prayers🙏 today and always.
Like • Reply • July 8 at 10:50am

Rach S.: God is bigger than all this and his mighty power has your family covered. Lots of prayers. Hugs and love🖤
Like • Reply • July 8 at 10:52am

Lisa W.: Unceasing prayer and love for all of you.
Like • Reply • July 8 at 11:05am

Alisha G.: sending love, strength and prayer...all day!!
Like • Reply • July 8 at 11:13am

Cassie M.: Praying for you guys today and everyday 🙏

Steve Riggs
July 8 • Phoenix, AZ •
Ok... So the results of the MRI are back... 4 days ago Paxton was found not breathing, no heartbeat. We were told after the initial CT scan to expect permanent and severe brain damage. Four days later the MRI has shown NO SEVERE DAMAGE. Now, there are areas of the brain that have been affected. So we don't have a clear bill of health by any means. But with a lot of rehab the doctors feel that even that damage may be reversed. We have a long road ahead of us. Lots of work for Paxton and us. But this is the biggest miracle we could have ever asked for! And it truly is a miracle. And I know it was partly due to your prayers, your love and your support. God is good. And friends, family and even strangers stepped up beyond our wildest expectations. I cannot express enough gratitude for you all. And I cannot express enough joy that we will be able to continue our journey through life with our little boy by our side. With love and prayer, anything is possible ❤🙏
Like • Comment • Share • 45 • Amber A., Judy H and 43 others 13 shares •Comments

Shannon D.: Goosebumps and tears! 👏
Like • Reply • July 8 at 12:06pm

Alisha G.: tears of joy!!!!! I'm SO HAPPY for all of you!!!! and I can not WAIT to meet that little miracle!
Like • Reply • 4 • July 8 at 12:10pm

Rhonda K.: Wonderful news!!!!! We will continue to lift you all up in prayer for the days and weeks ahead.
Like • Reply • 1 • July 8 at 12:13pm

Judy K.: OMG I am so grateful for God's hands in this miracle. Blessings and continued prayers for all of you.
Like • Reply • 1 • July 8 at 12:17pm

Meagan S.: This is such wonderful and amazing news, Steve! I'm tearing up with joy and relief for you. You and Deserae are strong

and loving parents and you've got two strong little girls who will help rally Paxton back to being the strong little boy he's used to being. Obviously that strength is already kicking in with all the progress he's made over these four days. You have an army of support and love behind you. I'm continuing to send love and healing thoughts your way. It's a long road ahead of you, but you have lots of us to lend a hand and loving support. If anyone can do this - it's your family. You are amazing. Love to you all.
Like • Reply • 1 • July 8 at 12:18pm

Justin F.: Great news! So happy for you all bro!
Like • Reply • July 8 at 12:23pm

Brad J.: Wonderful news. Very happy to hear this.
Like • Reply • July 8 at 12:27pm

Brigett L.: Tears of joys!!!!! Omg this is the best news!!!!!
Like • Reply • July 8 at 12:27pm

Kim P.: Thank you Jesus!!!!! God is so good!!!! I'm so happy to hear this news!!!!! Wow - amazing!
Like • Reply • July 8 at 12:28pm

Shannon J.: Thank god!!!!
Like • Reply • July 8 at 12:28pm

Desiree M.: Steve I cannot tell you how many patients I have had over the years that have defied all of the odds by the power of prayer/ meditation and pure will and determination! I have tears of joy for you my friend, stay positive and we will continue to keep you and Paxton in our thoughts and prayers
Like • Reply • July 8 at 12:29pm

Rob S.: God is so great! News has me all teary eyed. GO PAX!!!
Like • Reply • July 8 at 12:42pm

Joan T.: This is the most wonderful news, I'm so happy and relieved for you all! 😊☺️🖤
Like • Reply • July 8 at 1:01pm

Shelly S.: Praise the Lord! He IS good!! Love to you all!!!💖🙏👍
Like • Reply • July 8 at 1:34pm

Amber A.: So happy for this miracle!! God is good. Our prayers will continue as he continues to recover!
Like • Reply • July 8 at 1:35pm

Linda G.: wonderful news!!! will continue praying for him and your family!!
Like • Reply • July 8 at 1:40pm

Anne M.: This is amazing news! With God all things are possible.
Like • Reply • July 8 at 1:41pm

Anissa C.: High Five! Still sending prayers.
Like • Reply • July 8 at 1:42pm

Shanti W.: Way to go Paxton! <3
Like • Reply • July 8 at 1:43pm

Rach S.: Go PAX... We are cheering you on strong boy. God is right by your side with your guardian angels 💪😇
Like • Reply • July 8 at 1:50pm

Sean T.: So glad to hear this man! He's strong just like his daddy!
Like • Reply • July 8 at 1:54pm

Barry W.: Awesome! Wonderful news!
Like • Reply • July 8 at 2:04pm

Nancy B.: So happy to hear the good news, Paxton is in such good hands, in many ways. Thank you for sharing Steve, it means a lot to be able to follow his progress. He's a chip off the ole chainsaw, that's for sure!!
Like • Reply • July 8 at 2:36pm

Lisa M.: So great to read this! ☺ ☐
Like • Reply • July 8 at 2:51pm
Fred A.: That's so awesome!
Like • Reply • July 8 at 3:03pm

Mike Meg K.: Way to go little man!!! Keep it up.
Like • Reply • July 8 at 3:43pm

Tara G.: ❤❤❤!!!
Like • Reply • July 8 at 4:40pm

Diane M.: Praise God from whom all blessings flow!!!
Like • Reply • July 8 at 5:32pm

Liz G.: Oh sweet boy!!!! Love and prayers are still coming from us and everyone we know!
Like • Reply • 1 • July 8 at 5:59pm

Brian W.: Awesome, just freakin' awesome!
Like • Reply • July 8 at 7:48pm

Steve Riggs
July 8 • Phoenix, AZ •
Welcome back baby boy❤

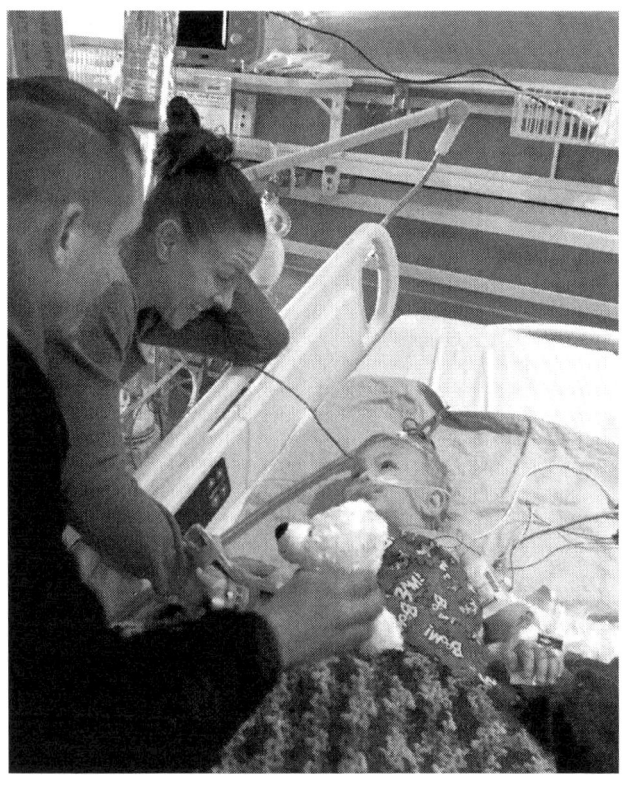

Like • Comment • Share • 63 • Kim P., Amber A. and 61 others 2 shares • Comments

Anne M.: My heart is so happy
Like • Reply • July 8 at 4:33pm

Loretta K.: Mine too..
Like • Reply • 1 • July 8 at 4:37pm

Rach S.: Exciting!!!! Yay
Like • Reply • July 8 at 4:38pm

Alisha G.: Ohhhhhh. This makes my day!!! My heart is so full for you guys!! 🌷
Like • Reply • July 8 at 4:38pm

Robt W.: Holy smokes. So exciting!
Like • Reply • July 8 at 4:39pm

Steve R.: He still doesn't really know who we are. So one step at a time. But we're just happy he's back.
Like • Reply • 5 • July 8 at 4:39pm

Anne M.: One step at a time, but we are still walking.
Like • Reply • 1 • July 8 at 4:41pm

Loretta K.: I see love in his eyes for you
Like • Reply • 1 • July 8 at 5:04pm

Tara G.: ❤❤❤!!!
Like • Reply • 1 • July 8 at 4:42pm

Lisa W.: So much going on in his little body! I'm sure he knows your love though!
Like • Reply • 1 • July 8 at 4:43pm

Steve T.: WOW, what a strong boy! Amazing and so happy to see this!
Like • Reply • 1 • July 8 at 4:43pm

Mike Meg K.: No words to explain our feelings right now. Tears shed in this Klinger home for your sweet boy. Please let us know of you need anything.
Like • Reply • July 8 at 4:52pm

Rob S.: So damn exciting!! The look of joy on y'all too! God bless Pax, you all, and all the medical staff that's helped him out!
Like • Reply • 1 • July 8 at 4:53pm

Justin F.: Awesome!!!
Like • Reply • July 8 at 4:53pm

Brad J.: YES! YES! YES!
Like • Reply • July 8 at 4:55pm

Shannon J.: Look at her smile!! ❤❤❤
Like • Reply • 1 • July 8 at 4:59pm

Matt S.: That is one of the best pictures I've ever seen. I'm so happy.
Like • Reply • July 8 at 5:14pm

Jami G.: ❤❤
Like • Reply • July 8 at 5:15pm

Joan T.: This is the most beautiful thing I have seen, look at those eyes ☺ welcome back Pax!!!
Like • Reply • July 8 at 5:18pm

Nate R.: My favorite picture. On the road to recovery.
Like • Reply • 1 • July 8 at 5:18pm

Rhonda K.: So incredibly happy for all of you!!!
Like • Reply • July 8 at 5:22pm

Anthony T.: Awesome
Like • Reply • July 8 at 5:29pm

Judy K.: Melt my heart.. welcome back buddy.
Like • Reply • July 8 at 5:34pm

Kerri C.: Your face is Everything Deserae!!!! I have waited to see you smile this week and today it's You that is bringing tears to my eyes. Tears of Joy, I love you friend
Like • Reply • 2 • July 8 at 5:39pm

Shannon D.: Best thing I've seen all day!! <3
Like • Reply • July 8 at 5:41pm

Myra A.-R.: Oh my goodness! Such a beautiful sight to see! 😊❤
Like • Reply • July 8 at 5:59pm

Nicole P.: Absolutely amazing! I'm so happy for Paxton and you all! Sending lots of love and joy your way!
Like • Reply • July 8 at 6:00pm

Jessica G.: Yay!!!! So happy for you guys!
Like • Reply • July 8 at 6:05pm

Nancy B.: What a joyous sight!
Like • Reply • July 8 at 6:15pm

Cassie M.: Awe what a beautiful moment! So happy for you guys ❤
Like • Reply • July 8 at 6:52pm

Brian W.: Wow, picture of the year! Framing that one for sure!! Hang in there little man!
Like • Reply • July 8 at 7:50pm

Mary S.: Thank the Lord! Love to see your beautiful smile Dez!
Like • Reply • 1 • July 9 at 2:19am

Julie R.: Brings tears to my eyes. God Blessed!
Like • Reply • July 9 at 12:19pm

Amy H.: I love this picture so much, especially your smile Dez! Keep fighting baby boy! ❤ Sending love to you all!
Like • Reply • July 10 at 12:23pm

Steve Riggs
July 9 • Phoenix, AZ •

Well last night was a little rough for poor Pax-aroo. I'm careful to use the term "rough", because no night or day will be "rough" compared to what he has already gone through. But after being on the sedation medications Fentanyl, Precedex, and morphine for over 4 days he was finally taken off all 3. So it was a night full of withdrawals. Agitation, disorientation, sleeplessness, crying, and spiking fevers. Paxton stayed the strong little man we knew he was and Dez did an amazing job of being part mom and part nurse. Comforting him and watching over him with a careful eye at the same time. Just some basic information we have on Pax's recovery: He does have movement in all four limbs. Yay! However, how coordinated he is with these movements is yet to be seen. He is still unable to follow simple commands such as "squeeze my finger". And he obviously is a long way from performing tasks such as feeding himself, crawling or walking. BUT he is strong, often giving the nurses all they bargained for trying to get readings or perform tests. As you have also noticed from our pictures he has opened his eyes as well. He can see and is sensitive to light. But he does not appear to recognize anyone at this point. However, he is able to be calmed by Deserae's and my voice. So there does seem to be some connect. He is also not talking, but he was always more of a "pointer and grunter" than a talker prior to the accident so that doesn't necessarily surprise me. Lol. But I will continue to fill you guys in on any additional progress he makes. And again, thanks to the prayer warriors, love and support. Love you guys.
Like • Comment • Share • 39 • Judy H., Diane M. and 37 others • Comments

Rach S.: Really appreciate all the updates. Pax has the best of both worlds, an awesome mom and an awesome nurse all in one ;)
Like • Reply • 3 • July 9 at 6:43am

Jami G.: Continued prayers for your family
Like • Reply • July 9 at 8:27am

Lisa M.: Ditto on what Rach said!
Like • Reply • 1 • July 9 at 9:01am

Nancy B.: Great way to start the day with lots of Paxton Progress. Love to all❤.
Like • Reply • July 9 at 9:14am

Adam Elizabeth G.: Continuing prayers while rejoicing In the early victories ❤
Like • Reply • July 9 at 9:59am

Justin F.: Continued prayers every day for your boy!
Like • Reply • July 9 at 10:13am

Steve Riggs
July 9 • Phoenix, AZ •
Hey, you look familiar ❤❤

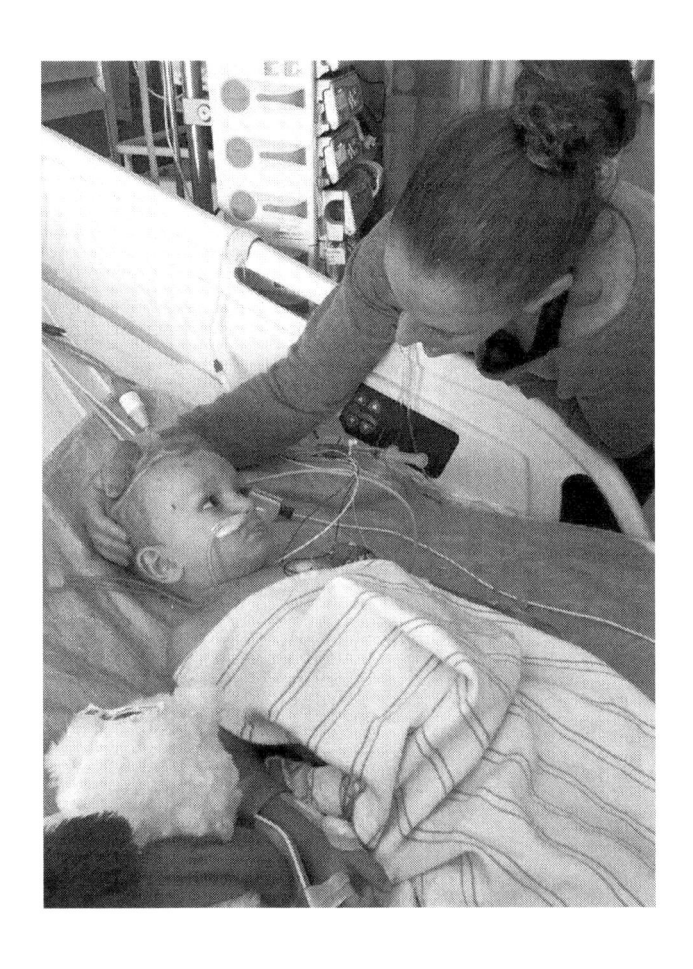

Like • Comment • Share • 53 Loretta K., Amber A. and 51 others •
Comments

Rach S.: Aww...so sweet
Like • Reply • July 9 at 8:42am

Kerri C.: Good morning baby♥♥♥
Like • Reply • July 9 at 8:54am

Rob S.: Love it!
Like • Reply • July 9 at 9:01am

Anissa C.: Now tell mom you want ice cream! I'm so happy for all of you.
Like • Reply • July 9 at 9:04am

Travis K. Bri A.: Love you Pax!!
Like • Reply • July 9 at 10:29am

Judy K.: Fantastic!
Like • Reply • July 9 at 11:19am

Kim P.: Precious boy ☺
Like • Reply • July 9 at 11:54am

Etta M.: Praying for speedy and full recovery for Paxton.
Like • Reply • July 9 at 2:27pm

Steve Riggs
July 9 • Phoenix, AZ •
Tonight's update: Honestly I don't even know where to start. First I want to apologize to any friends I was unable to get back to. Today was extremely hard for me, and of course more importantly, Paxton. Today since he was out of sedation he is going through something called "Neuro Storming". I would not wish this on any person. Or any loved one to have to watch. It is essentially when the brain is injured and trying to heal and every neuron in their brain is firing all at once. It resembles seizures that are occurring a majority of the time. Spastic motions. And even moments of no breathing. We still haven't been able to hold him and he's back on some medications. Now, this can be a normal process of the brain healing. It apparently isn't necessarily a setback. But it is both heart breaking and horrifying to watch. Especially when it's your baby boy. I have always known this is a process. I was not prepared enough for today. However, this does not shake my faith. And Dez and the rest of my family stepped in when my strength was shaken. Tomorrow is a new day. And even if it presents the same challenges or even new ones we will NOT give up! We have seen Gods miracle, He is present. We have seen Paxton's strength, he is fighting. So we must too. And if I can I would like to ask you all for the prayers to continue. You all are part of this. A part of our story. Our miracle. Thank you. ❤️🙏

Like • Comment • Share • 38 • Nancy B., Kim P. and 35 others •
Comments

Rach S.: Awe that's rough... Especially seeing your baby having a hard time and you can't fix it for him. He is going to get through this. You guys are such awesome parents who are Paxton's strength. Keep pushing over this hurdle... God is caring you though your weakness. Def praying all the time for you guys and Paxton. So proud of you guys. Much love and prayers.
Like • Reply • July 9 at 7:56pm

Rob S.: Steve bro, won't give up praying of course. There's gonna be good days and bad days, but every bad day for Pax's recovery here with us is still a good day! Love you guys man. Get some rest so you can be ready for tomorrow.
Like • Reply • 1 • July 9 at 8:05pm • Edited

Meagan S.: I'm sorry, Steve. That sounds so difficult. You are surrounded by love and strength. Today you leaned on family. Another day you will be there to support others. Every day you are allowing Paxton to lean on you. Hang in there. Sending love and healing thoughts. Keeping you and your family in my heart.
Like • Reply • 1 • July 9 at 8:04pm

Loretta K.: Bless your Hearts, Steve, Dez, AND PAXTON.. SO SORRY you have go through this.. I'm glad you are strong hearted and strong minded... love you
Like • Reply • July 9 at 8:17pm

Jenna S.: Love you guys!
Like • Reply • July 9 at 9:21pm

Ana G.: One day at a time Steven! He's come a long a way! God is good! We'll keep praying! ❤❤
Like • Reply • July 9 at 11:18pm

Linda G.: praying for your family and Pax always n every day! know you will stay strong for him!! and thanks for updates cause you're in my heart always ❤
Like • Reply • July 10 at 12:15am

Jessica G.: Thank you for the consistent updates. We all appreciate it so much. I'm constantly praying for little Paxton and for God to grant you & the girls strength through this journey.
Like • Reply • July 10 at 12:27am

Tara G.: Prayers for strength only His love and guidance can give you...stay present and keep looking to Him...and know we are doing the same and rooting for y'all! 👨‍👩‍👧‍👦📖💜
Like • Reply • July 10 at 12:34am

Joan T.: Prayers are still coming, for not only your baby boy but for all of you having to watch helplessly by as your boy struggles to recover. Hugs and love to you all, and of course prayers as well
Like • Reply • July 10 at 7:27am • Edited

Sheryl C.: We are here. Hang in there. You have the love and support of an amazing "family". Prayers are constant with us and for you.
Like • Reply • 1 • July 10 at 7:22am

Steve Riggs added 15 new photos.
July 10 • Gilbert, AZ •
Sometimes you don't post every picture because you don't want to be "that dad". But I'm posting them now... More pics from the wonderful personalities of the boy we call Pax.

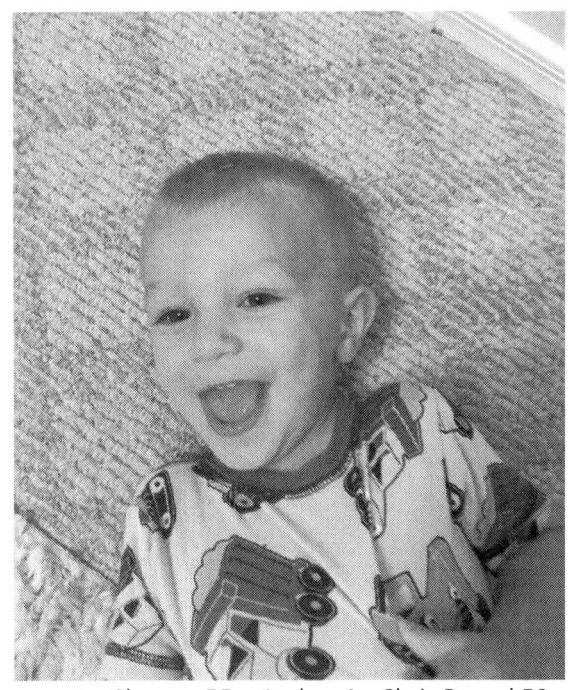

Like • Comment • Share • 55 • Amber A., Chris R. and 52 others 1 share • Comments

Nancy B.: And I'm glad you did. He gave me a big smile this morning. Hope today is a little better than yesterday. Such a cutie.
Like • Reply • July 10 at 7:38am

Kim P.: Love these!!!
Like • Reply • July 10 at 8:23am

Shon P. Outstanding bro, your hair is getting long dude!
Like • Reply • July 10 at 9:32am

Cassie M.: ❤
Like • Reply • July 10 at 11:33am

Steve Riggs
July 10 • Phoenix, AZ •
So it looks like the medical team is hooking him back up to the EEG machine today (analyzes brain activity). They are trying to determine how much of his behavior is "Neuro Storming" and if some of it are seizures. He now only has a blank stare. No eye tracking or awareness. It was also explained to us that just because the first MRI looked good, that some of that brain tissue still may die. Conversely, this can still possibly be part of the Neuro storming and part of the healing process. And a full recovery is not out of the question. So much uncertainty. So many questions that cannot be answered. It appears that we will be in pediatric ICU for quite some time. And now the balance between focusing on the care of Paxton while remembering we have two other beautiful kids that need their mom and dad starts. The overall health of Paxton will obviously be our main concern, but it will be a balancing act nonetheless. Sometimes I wonder if I write these posts as updates, or as therapy for myself. Probably both. But thanks for listening. And thanks for the support. ❤️🙏
Like • Comment • Share • 38 Loretta K., Kim P. and 35 others 1 share • Comments

Travis K. Bri A. We love you guys so much and will always be there to support you!
Like • Reply • July 10 at 8:45am

Brian W.: Sometimes life takes a village Steve, remember that, though I'm sure it obvious. Your village is ready to go! Lean on them for that stuff they can do, focus on what you only can do.
Like • Reply • 4 • July 10 at 8:51am

Deana P.: Praying for his healing. If you need help with the girls I'm here or anything else you guys need.
Like • Reply • July 10 at 8:53am

Sheryl C.: A long road ahead, no doubt. Lace up those boots, you can do it. The love of family and friends will help you through. We all are going to keep constant vigil with prayer and positive thoughts. Your beautiful girls are getting a tough yet strong lesson in love, family, and faith. You and Dez can do this and together you will learn to juggle just fine. *hugs*
Like • Reply • 1 • July 10 at 8:58am

Jami G.: Continued prayers for your family 🙏
Like • Reply • July 10 at 9:05am

Rach S.: Love your updates. Thanks for keeping us all in the loop as we pray and know more specifics to pray on ;). Remember don't let what good God is doing let satan distract you. He will do whatever it takes to distract you. Know God is bigger than all this. Love you guys and keep the updates coming no matter what they are and we will keep praying.
Like • Reply • 1 • July 10 at 9:14am

Meagan S.: We are grateful for the updates. And, I think you are right - they are both for your family of love and support and for your peace of mind. We are here to lift you up - whether near or far. Let the juggling begin. You and Dez can do this. And you have family and friends to help share the load. Keeping you in our hearts and sending more love than can be imagined.
Like • Reply • 4 • July 10 at 9:27am

Ana G.: It's a long road for you both! But your family and friends are all here to help support you all! The girls love there baby brother and would do anything for him!! God is good & is continuing to help Paxton & everyone through this! Always thinking of you guys!!❤❤❤
Like • Reply • July 10 at 9:28am

Anne M.: This isn't a sprint, it is one small step at a time. The brain is such an unknown, it's unpredictable and astonishing. There will be steps backwards, and it's difficult not to get discouraged. Just keep the faith. Keep taking care of yourself. Keep taking care of your children. Just keep taking those small steps. And while you all take those steps, we will be supporting you and loving you through this, because that is what family does.

Like • Reply • 4 • July 10 at 12:06pm • Edited

Stephanie Z.: I'm sure it's both but please keep updating. We all want to know how all of you are doing.
Like • Reply • July 10 at 9:42am

Nancy B.: There's not much more I can add Steve that your friends and family haven't already said. But do appreciate your thinking of us with your posts. Sending you all hugs and prayers.
Like • Reply • July 10 at 9:43am

Fred A.: Thanks for all of the updates and stay strong
Like • Reply • July 10 at 9:49am

Loretta K.: Thanks for these updates.. I am constantly thinking and praying for you..
Like • Reply • 1 • July 10 at 9:54am

Liz D.: I have been checking Facebook I think on average every 2 to 3 minutes for updates. Constantly praying for u all.
Like • Reply • July 10 at 10:21am

Nicole P.: Sending lots of love and prayers your way!
Like • Reply • July 10 at 10:22am

Desiree M.: Exactly what they said! You are an amazing dad no matter what! Thank you for updating and we continue to pray for healing
Like • Reply • July 10 at 11:20am

Amber A.: Your WA/OR family appreciate all the updates. Others have said it well - near or far we are all here to support you. Being far, we continue to pray for you all. Thank you for including us in the ups and downs.
Like • Reply • July 10 at 12:40pm

Elizabeth D.: We are there with you Steve, maybe not physically but for sure emotionally, so continue with the updates so we don't have to bother you, and know our prayers continue to come your way. 🙏🙏🙏
Like • Reply • July 11 at 10:03am

Steve Riggs
July 10 at 11:01am • Phoenix, AZ •
So as I mentioned, we still haven't been able to hold Paxton. So when the nurse stepped away Dez crawled into bed next to him. So then she told ME too. Although I barely fit with Pax and all his cords I got to hold and kiss my little boy. He woke up long enough to yawn and look around the room a little. He even turned his head to look at me (although he still has no idea who I am). But it was a small victory. And man it felt good! It's just what I needed after the past couple days. Love you Pax-aroo!!!!❤❤❤
Like • Comment • Share • 54 Amber A, Kim P. and 51 others 1 share • Comments

Steve R. ❤🙈

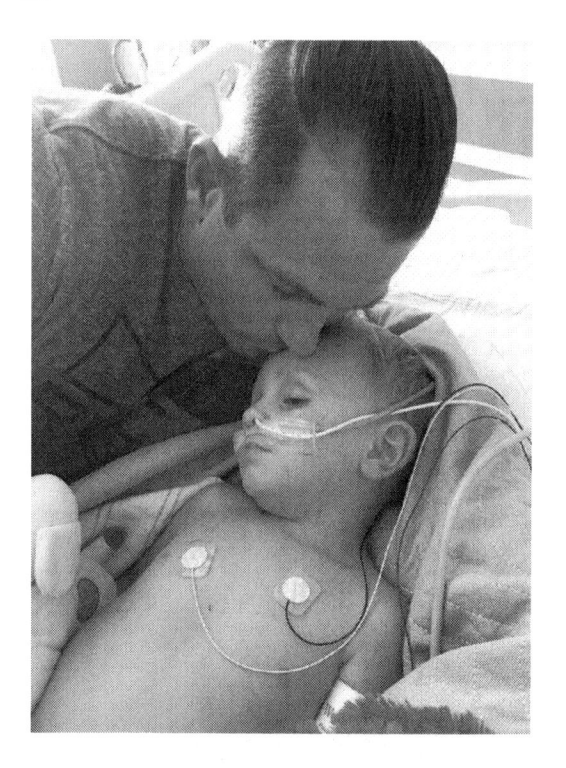

Like • Reply • 15 • July 10 at 11:04am

Rach S.: Awe that's the best. Love this
Like • Reply • July 10 at 11:12am

Rob S.: Such an awesome thing. I remember when I was in my hospital bed and Rach and the kids would crawl in with me. Def just what I needed, and I know it's just what y'all needed too!
Like • Reply • 1 • July 10 at 11:19am

Jenna S.: Yay! Must've been the best feeling!
Like • Reply • July 10 at 11:24am

Liz D.: ❤❤❤❤❤❤
Like • Reply • July 10 at 11:29am

Ana G.: 😲😲❤❤
Like • Reply • July 10 at 11:38am

Alisha G.: His brain might not know who you guys are...But his heart does.....so happy you all got a little snuggle in....❤
Like • Reply • 2 • July 10 at 12:28pm

Steve Riggs
July 10 at 2:54pm • Phoenix, AZ •

So now I'm officially bordering on TOO MANY updates but this next one will be worth it. As I mentioned earlier Dez and I both crawled in bed with Paxton. After the first time and during the second time he became much more alert... And for the first time he looked at us and smiled. Then came a giggle. Now these events of his increased alertness and emotion lasted for maybe 5-10 minutes each and then he returned to a sedated state. But to see my baby boy smile for the first time and hear his laugh brought tears to my eyes. We still have a long way to go and with every step forward sometimes comes with a step backwards. So I will curb my enthusiasm just a little until this becomes a pattern of continued improvement. But for this moment I will enjoy it. I will LOVE it. My little boy and his infectious little smile was back. ❤️👶

Like • Comment • Share • 53 Katie R., Kim P. and 50 others •
Comments

Rob S.: EPIC! Such greatness!
Like • Reply • July 10 at 2:57pm

Anne M.: Fantastic news!!! These small steps give the greatest reward.
Like • Reply • July 10 at 2:58pm

Liz D.: Tears r rolling!!!! That's huge!!! Moments like these will get u thru!!
Like • Reply • July 10 at 2:59pm

Stephanie Z.: It will never be too many updates, please keep them coming! I'm so happy you are having some good moments between the bad.
Like • Reply • July 10 at 3:04pm

Diane M.: Thank you for sharing Steve, we love you!
Like • Reply • July 10 at 3:05pm

Loretta K.: Oh Steve.. Tears of JOY.. VERY EPIC..
Like • Reply • July 10 at 3:11pm

Amber F.: There will never be too many updates ... Ever!
Like • Reply • 1 • July 10 at 3:14pm

Loretta K.: I agree
Like • Reply • July 10 at 3:15pm

Joshua D.: keep em coming brother!!!
Like • Reply • July 10 at 3:19pm

Jessica G.: You can never update too much! :) praying these happy moments continue and become more frequent!
Like • Reply • 3 • July 10 at 3:24pm

Kim P.: Love the updates!!! Keep em coming!
Like • Reply • July 10 at 3:34pm

Brian W.: Steve, if they are good for you, keep um coming. They are wonderful for us, but we would all understand. Great news, smiles=good!
Like • Reply • 1 • July 10 at 3:41pm

Brigett L.: Never never too many updates!! Thank you so much for taking us on this journey with you! You are always on our mind we are there with you in spirit!
Like • Reply • 1 • July 10 at 3:42pm

Desiree M.: Never too much! I love it 💗💗💗
Like • Reply • July 10 at 3:54pm

Rach S.: Awe that's so awesome. Love to hear this. Best healing he can have is a parents love. Keep it up ;)
Like • Reply • 1 • July 10 at 4:03pm

Jenna S.: I'd like them hourly until I can't be there tomorrow. ☺ thanks. Hope you holding him is next!!!!
Like • Reply • July 10 at 4:10pm • Edited

Lisa M.: Love it! 💖 So awesome ☺ ☐
Like • Reply • 1 • July 10 at 4:13pm

Meagan S.: Can't ever post too many updates. What a wonderful post!
Like • Reply • July 10 at 5:09pm

Sheryl C.: Love should be a prescribed therapy. So very happy for you.🖤
Like • Reply • 1 • July 10 at 6:33pm

Shelly S.: Never too many updates! We love hearing what's going on whether it's good, not so good whatever! It helps us know how to specifically pray!!🙇💝 †
Like • Reply • July 10 at 7:35pm

Nancy B.: So good to hear, never hesitate to share with us - love to hear the news!!
Like • Reply • July 10 at 9:44pm

Etta M.: God is so good, hold on to your Faith and know he loves your family and will be with you through it all.
Like • Reply • July 11 at 5:08pm

Steve Riggs
July 11 at 7:49am • Phoenix, AZ •

Update: After a full week in ICU Pax is finally stable (crossing our fingers he stays that way). He was put on 2 meds for the Neuro Storming and 1 med for seizures. He has been weened down to the smallest dose of sedative he can receive and there is little doubt he will be off of that early this morning. His oxygen (nasal cannula) is being weened as well. And soon he will have that removed. The EEG has done its job in determining what is going on with the storming and seizures so that will be remove. So that will leave the feeding tube and femoral (groin) IV. We're guessing he will meet with the Speech Therapist today to see if he can swallow correctly so they can introduce real food and get rid of the feeding tube. But he's already trying to eat the toothpaste they are giving him and putting things in his mouth so that's a good sign. So that leaves the neurological aspect and physical rehab. They say for every day in bed expect 3 days to be able to recover physically. He has been in bed almost 8 days... So even if he left today (and he's not close to leaving) he would be looking at almost a month until he's back on his feet. As far as the brain injury. He seems to be coming to. He's able to visually track people. Dez and I are able to calm him, and he is able to express emotion. Unfortunately he still doesn't fully recognize anyone. He can't follow commands such as "squeeze my finger", "hold my hand", or "wave"(he used to wave and say hi to EVERYONE). Initially he was very disoriented and seemed very confused and scared. And although he still seems to display these characteristics, they are diminishing slightly, and at times our eyes connect and I see Paxton in there. A spark, a connection.
Something only a parent could recognize. This is still a journey. But I STRONGLY believe that my faith in God and the support of you all has provided a "miracle". Don't get me wrong, Paxton has received THE BEST medical care I have EVER seen. The team here at Phoenix Children's Hospital is AMAZING. But I honestly feel that there is an element to this story that was a miracle. That can't be explained by medical science. And I know I'll lose a few of you when I start talking about religion or faith. But it's something I feel to my core.

And it's part of the story I want to tell. My new motto. Love and faith... Anything is possible. 💜🙏
Like • Comment • Share • 56 Amber A., Kim P. and 53 others •
Comments

Rach S.: Amen... This is your guys God story. Love it. Praying everyday for y'all
Like • Reply • July 11 at 8:33am

Shelly S.: Happy for the progress! I know it's going to take time so I'm praying for continued healing and patience for all involved, especially Pax!! Love you guys!!💜🙏👍
Like • Reply • July 11 at 8:33am

Steve R.: I just noticed a spell issue. I accidentally put he *can hold your hand, squeeze finger, wave. Unfortunately it was supposed to say *can't Do those things. But regardless he is still making good progress
Like • Reply • July 11 at 8:44am

Stephanie Z.: Again thank you for these updates. I'm so happy to read this update today and I agree, there is definitely a miracle happening ☺
Like • Reply • July 11 at 8:51am

Ana G.: I'm glad to hear he's making some progress! Babysteps! #PraiseGod 💜💜💜
Like • Reply • July 11 at 9:29am

Adam Elizabeth G.: God is good. Love the updates!!! Still praying 💜
Like • Reply • July 11 at 9:30am

Desiree M.: This is wonderful news! And I do believe in a miraculous recovery i have witnessed it before. stay strong sweetie, keep that faith love and hope ☺
Like • Reply • July 11 at 10:32am

Cathy V.: Amen!
Like • Reply • July 11 at 11:31am

Cassie M.: Amazing! I completely agree...along with a strong willed boy and loving parents by his side ❤
Like • Reply • July 11 at 1:54pm

Braidon F.: Thank you for the update! Such amazing news! :)
Like • Reply • July 11 at 2:09pm

Anissa C.: Amen! Im happy for you all.
Like • Reply • July 11 at 2:21pm

Lisa M.: Love reading the updates! Continued prayers and hugs to all of you! ❤
Like • Reply • 1 • July 11 at 2:29pm

Mary S.: Amazing, so happy to hear the good updates.
Like • Reply • July 11 at 6:13pm

Judy K.: All that love from Mom and Dad, miracle workers at the hospital, Paxton fighting, and Divine intervention, for sure. Great update.
Like • Reply • July 11 at 6:29pm

Tara G.: Stay strong and true to your ❤&faith Riggsy...your honesty and grace through adversity will speak to many...XO
Like • Reply • July 11 at 9:09pm

Steve Riggs
July 11 at 12:01pm • Phoenix, AZ •
Just a momma and her boy❤

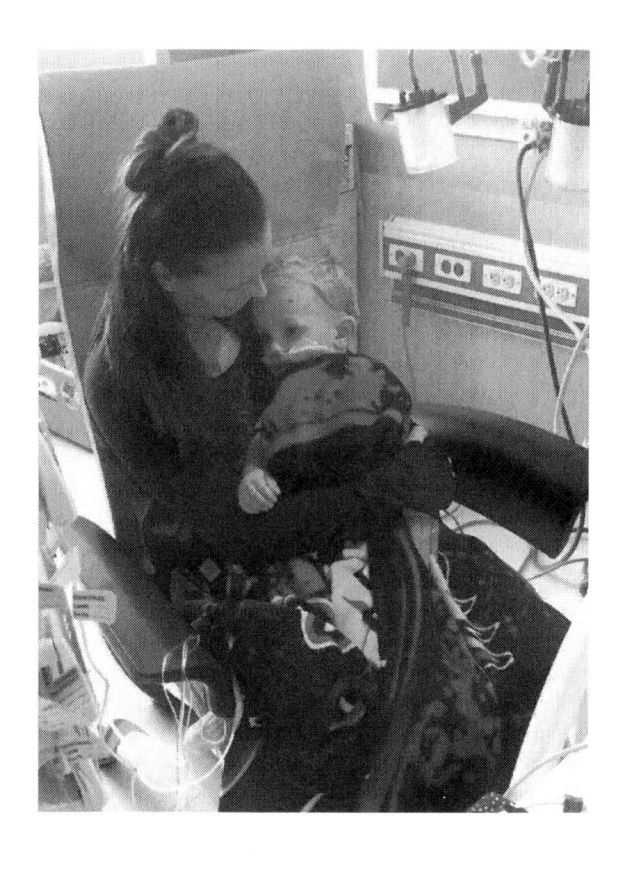

Like • Comment • Share • 64 Nancy B., Amber A. and 62 others •
Comments

Stephanie Z.: Beautiful ☺ thank you for sharing.
Like • Reply • July 11 at 12:13pm

Jenna S.: Yaaaaasssssss!
Like • Reply • July 11 at 12:14pm

Judy K.: Finally in your arms!
Like • Reply • July 11 at 12:16pm

Steve T.: 😊😊😊😊 such an amazing picture! Happy to see this
Like • Reply • July 11 at 12:22pm

Rhonda K.: Great medicine for mom and for Pax!
Like • Reply • 1 • July 11 at 12:26pm

Shelly S.: That's the BEST medicine ... Mommie & boy!!!
Like • Reply • July 11 at 12:42pm

Loretta K.: Awwwwww
Like • Reply • July 11 at 12:51pm

Mike Meg K.: BEAUTIFUL!
Like • Reply • July 11 at 12:56pm

Rach S.: Precious.
Like • Reply • July 11 at 12:59pm

Shannon J.: Yay!!!
Like • Reply • July 11 at 1:05pm

Cathy V.: Love it!!! So precious!
Like • Reply • July 11 at 1:27pm

Ana G.: What a blessing!
Like • Reply • July 11 at 1:32pm

Alisha G.: yay! oh i bet she is so happy! :)
Like • Reply • July 11 at 1:59pm

Amy H.: So happy you finally get to hold your baby, Dez! 🖤🖤
Like • Reply • July 11 at 2:23pm

Etta M.: The best medicine for a little boy is mommy. He is in the arms of his Angel. Prays for healing.
Like • Reply • July 11 at 2:50pm

Donna B.: Awesome--another baby step in the right direction. Sitting in Mom's lap is very healing.
Like • Reply • July 11 at 3:29pm

Steve Riggs
July 11 at 7:28pm • Phoenix, AZ •

Tonight's update will be short. Basically the medical staff did pretty much everything I thought they would. Discontinued the rest of Pax's sedation meds. Removed him from oxygen. And started him on physical, occupational and speech therapy. And after tomorrow's antibiotics they will remove all IVs (he only actually has a femoral one left). He will remain on all anti-seizure and Neuro storming meds for probably at least 6 months. Being the crazy dad I am I envisioned all 3 "rehabs" to go much better though. Speech therapy he was able to eat but they noticed some abnormalities in his swallowing so he is scheduled for a swallow study tomorrow to find out why. Occupational he just has no desire (or maybe ability?) to pick things up and is delayed in several motor skills. And physical therapy (his best) he was able to pretty much able to hold himself in a sitting position as long as someone assisted with head control. But he really tired out quickly. Today it finally hit me how many months (if not years) it will take him to get back to where he was. So long story short (ok maybe this wasn't a "short update") it looks like we will be out of ICU soon (Yay!!). But we will probably be transferred to the in-center rehab floor for quite some time. ❤️

Like • Comment • Share • 51 Nancy B., Amber A. and 49 others 1 share • Comments

Brian W.: Progress is excellent, think of how much of our lives we spend just staying in the same place....one step forward, one day at a time!
Like • Reply • 1 • July 11 at 7:30pm

Mike S.: Praying for him daily bud.
Like • Reply • July 11 at 7:38pm

Loretta K.: Oh Steve and Dez. He has excelled in everything so far... I'm praying my sweet children....
Like • Reply • July 11 at 8:01pm

Rach S.: Dude, for being dead to being where he is now... He is doing awesome. One day at a time my friend. As a parent though you want it now, that's totally understandable. He will get there. The lord will be teaching lots of patients ;). Love you guys and so proud of you both
Like • Reply • 2 • July 11 at 8:11pm

Amy H.: He will come back, I know he will, he is such a strong little boy! You are in my thoughts & prayers every day, love you all! ♥
Like • Reply • July 11 at 8:29pm

Steve R.: Rach, I rarely respond to comments under my updates. Not because I don't value everyone. It's just that I feel if I respond to everyone than I'm robbing Pax of the attention he needs by being on the internet all day. But I will respond to this one. And it's a 100% you're absolutely right. I find myself discouraged when progress or prognosis doesn't turn out exactly how I want it to. But then I'll have a flashback of Dez's voice when I answered the phone that night to her screaming and sobbing "Paxton's dead! Paxton's dead!!!". It is a voice and a moment I will never ever ever forget. And then it slaps the hell out of me back into reality. How fortunate I am. And how grateful for every second I should be. Ironically today was the first time since that night that we had that same Doctor taking care of us. The one that told us Paxton was going to die or have severe brain damage. Usually the Docs stand outside our room and take "daily rounds". She walked right past her colleagues, into our room, shook her head in disbelief and said "incredible ". Now THAT'S amazing. When your child defies the odds to where the Doctors are in disbelief. So you're right. Sometimes I just need a little bit of clarify.
Like • Reply • 15 • July 11 at 8:34pm • Edited

Ana G.: Steven Life is precious & sometimes we take that for granted! But you have a second chance with your baby boy it's only natural for you to want everything to go your way! But One Day Your Baby Boy we'll be back to his old self!
#Godisgood❤❤❤👣Praying for you always!

Like • Reply • 1 • July 11 at 8:47pm • Edited

Rach S.: I totally never expect you to respond especially with everything you have going on. Your priority is that little boy and we are here to just love on you and be here for your needs. Thanks for sharing about that Doctor.... That is way cool. When this is all back to normal... You guys watch out.., God will be using you in some awesome way!!!!
Like • Reply • 1 • July 11 at 8:43pm

Shannon J.: Small victories.
Like • Reply • July 11 at 8:56pm

Jessica G.: Praying for every step. Both metaphorically and physically. We are all here cheering you ALL on. Not just Paxton. But you (steve), dez & the girls.
Like • Reply • July 12 at 12:08am

Dennis S.: Steve, you'll spent your entire life taking care of Paxton in one way or another - just as you will for your girls, as well - and just as it is for every family member, taking care of the others. It never ends, sometimes are just more challenging than others.
Like • Reply • July 12 at 12:21am

Dennis S.: And I want a response! If you respond to one, you must respond to all, no playing favorites! ;-) And I do hope you know I'm kidding!
Like • Reply • July 12 at 12:24am

Steve Riggs
July 12 at 6:26am • Phoenix, AZ •
Good morning family and friends!❤🤕

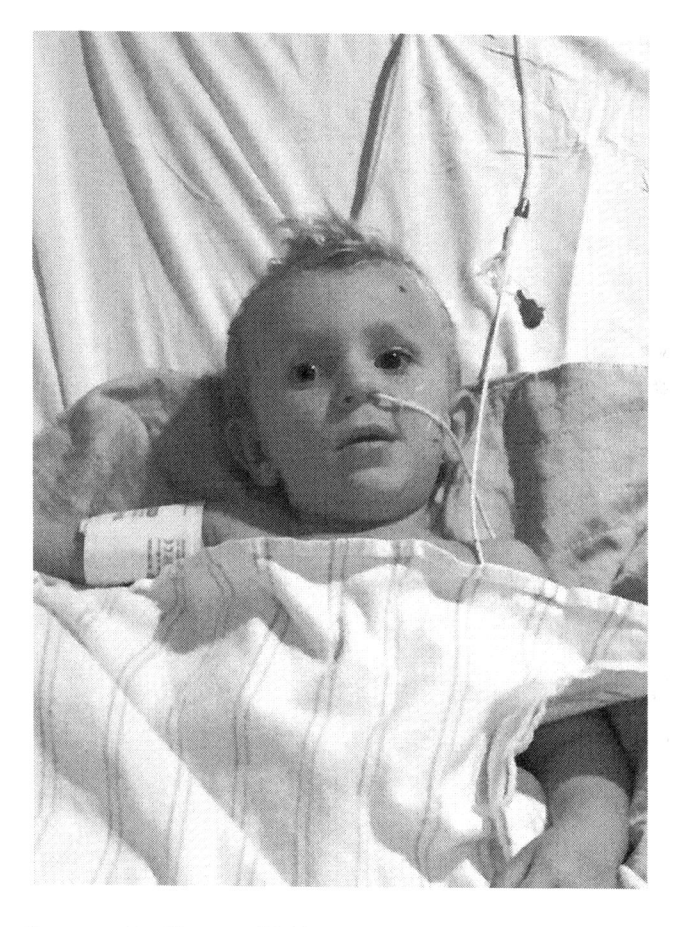

Like • Comment • Share • 58 Nancy B., Loretta K. and 55 others 2 shares • Comments

Brian W.: He looks wonderful, I look like crap when I wake up with a hose in my nose!
Like • Reply • 1 • July 12 at 6:28am

Stephanie Z.: ❤️😊
Like • Reply • July 12 at 6:34am

Matt S.: ☺
Like • Reply • July 12 at 6:38am

Rach S.: Omg he is looking a lot better. Such a cutie pie
Like • Reply • July 12 at 6:45am

Steve T.: 👍 👍
Like • Reply • July 12 at 6:45am

Shelly S.: He really is looking a lot better. Hope he continues to feel better!!
Like • Reply • July 12 at 7:15am

Mike Meg K.: Good morning sweet boy!
Like • Reply • July 12 at 7:50am

Judy K.: Hey handsome, Aunt Judy thinks you look awesome, your cousin Cy says you have bed head though!
Like • Reply • July 12 at 8:29am

Ana G.: Amazing!!He looks great! I'm so happy to see him & his beautiful eyes!❤️❤️👣
Like • Reply • July 12 at 8:30am • Edited

Liz G.: Well Hello Little Boy! Glad to see those eyes open and alert!!!
Like • Reply • July 12 at 10:12am

Noelle G.: God bless you sweet baby! You and your family are in my prayers.
Like • Reply • July 12 at 11:27am

Dennis S.: WOW! Steve, he doesn't even look like anything happened! Incredible! Well, aside from the NG tube and since I just

had one for 24 hours for an acid test, I don't even think that looks weird. Uncomfortable, yes (ugh, I remember it well). He looks super fantastic!
Like • Reply • July 12 at 1:17pm

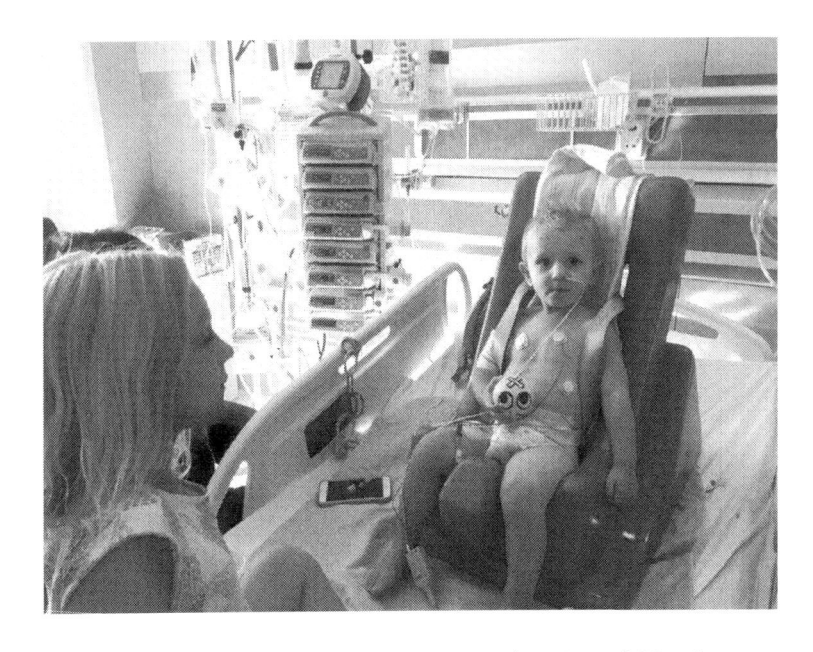

Steve Riggs
July 12 at 8:08am • Phoenix, AZ •
Brooklyn, our future physical therapist

Like • Comment • Share • 56 Nancy B., Amber A. and 53 others •
Comments

Rach S.: You girls with all the medical in your family will def be in the field ;)
Like • Reply • July 12 at 8:09am

Anissa C.: Good job! She's doing what a big sis should do. Her job is just being. Lol what until high school, you go girl.
Like • Reply • July 12 at 8:31am • Edited

Ana G.: Good Job sister! There his strength!!!☺👪❤❤#Priceless
Like • Reply • 1 • July 12 at 8:32am

Stephanie Z.: He is looking so good 😃
Like • Reply • July 12 at 9:15am

Desiree M.: Great profession 👏
Like • Reply • July 12 at 10:26am

Myra A.-R.: So precious 💖🙏📿
Like • Reply • July 12 at 10:32am

Rhonda K.: Those sisters will be amazing therapy helpers!
Like • Reply • July 12 at 11:24am

Dennis S.: You guys will all play a part in his recovery!
Like • Reply • July 12 at 1:12pm

Amber A.: He looks good in his little chair! Playing with big sis most definitely better than boring old PT/OT!! 😊

Steve Riggs
July 12 at 11:46am • Phoenix, AZ •
Always my little man❤️🧸

Like • Comment • Share • 68 Amber A., Kim P. and 66 others • Comments

Shelly S.: I bet that little man feels mighty good in your arms!!
Like • Reply • July 12 at 11:47am

Ana G.: #Amen Priceless beautiful picture I'm glad your finally holding him!!😊😮
Like • Reply • July 12 at 11:58am

Stephanie Z.: Happy daddy right there!
Like • Reply • July 12 at 12:05pm

Alisha G.: Yay! He sure looks like he knows you guys now! ❤
Like • Reply • July 12 at 1:25pm

Rach S.: Awe that's sweet. ☺
Like • Reply • July 12 at 1:59pm

Nancy B.: And he always will be!
Like • Reply • July 12 at 3:43pm

Elizabeth D.: Perfect picture, so glad you can hold him. 👨‍👩‍👧‍👦❤❤
Like • Reply • July 12 at 4:19pm

Nicole P.: So happy to see you smile! Amazing!! Pax sure is a little miracle!
Like • Reply • July 12 at 4:58pm

Steve Riggs
July 12 at 5:00pm • Phoenix, AZ •

Pax is asleep so it's safe to give today's update I suppose. Today Pax got moved from the Pediatric ICU to the neurology floor. And after talking with the doctor a few minutes ago it sounds like they are convinced he is so medically stable he will only be on the Neuro floor a day or two and then get transferred to the rehabilitation floor (the last stop before discharge). Once he's there we expect to be there for anywhere from a few weeks to 12 weeks (knowing Pax, if I was a betting man I'm putting my money on the lower end). Insurance will probably play a role in the duration as well. Anyway, he also passed his "swallow study" with flying colors so he will be back eating solid foods tomorrow, and in a couple days have his feeding tube removed (his LAST wire, IV, or tube... Yay!). His physical rehab this morning was a little discouraging. But when we put him to bed tonight on his back, he rolled over and got on his hands and knees by himself which was HUGE. This little man inspires me. He is so strong. So resilient. He has never once stopped fighting since this happened. And with the prayers of you all and the grace of God is doing things that amaze me. Way to go baby boy! Da-da is so proud of you! ❤️👶

Like • Comment • Share • 64 Katie R., Amber A. and 61 others •

Comments

Rach S.: Yay Pax. Strong boy. We look forward to the updates. 😊👶
Like • Reply • July 12 at 5:10pm

Adam Elizabeth G.: Go Pax!!!!
Like • Reply • July 12 at 5:16pm

Ana G.: #Amen #PraiseGod Go Baby boy! One day at time! That's all it takes pretty soon he'll be able to walk again! And get to go home!!👶👶Hugs and kisses!!
Like • Reply • July 12 at 5:26pm

Mike Meg K.: Great job little man. You are kicking ass....
Like • Reply • July 12 at 5:44pm

Rhonda K.: Thanks for all the updates!
Like • Reply • July 12 at 5:47pm

Richie R.: So happy to hear this news. Thanks for the updates. We continue to keep Pax in our prayers everyday!
Like • Reply • July 12 at 5:59pm

Brian W.: Awesome news, bad pun to say 'baby steps', but that little dude is knocking of some man size steps no doubt! Congrats Mom and Dad....keep your spirits up-the village will do the rest.
Like • Reply • July 12 at 7:18pm

Loretta K.: Grandma is so PROUD OF PAX
Like • Reply • July 12 at 7:26pm

Elizabeth D.: Wonderful news! Hang in there Steve, you are doing great. Pax will continue to amaze you, he is a little miracle.
Like • Reply • July 12 at 9:02pm

Meagan S.: This makes my heart so happy! I have to say, I check for your update the first thing in the morning and last thing before bed (and about ten times during the day). I'm so happy for you! Work through the hard days, cherish the peaceful moments and know that your love and determination will carry all five of you through. Love to you all.
Like • Reply • 5 • July 12 at 9:46pm

Loretta K.: Well said
Like · Reply · 1 · July 12 at 10:25pm

Judy K.: This is a HUGE update. Go PAX Go! Time to take a deep breath mom and dad! What a fighter!
Like • Reply • 1 • July 13 at 7:30am

Shelly S.: Any updates today??? How was his night?
Like • Reply • July 13 at 2:34pm

Steve Riggs
July 13 at 8:19pm • Phoenix, AZ •
Nightly update, Day 10: I think the days of "huge" developments are over. But Paxton is still making GREAT strides. Today he ate pancakes, eggs, hash browns, mac-n-cheese, bananas, yogurt, ravioli, JELL-O and 16 ounces of water/juice. Apparently he missed food. He did excellent at physical therapy rolling over, getting into a sitting position by himself and being able to balance without assistance. He was also able to get into a crawling position and with assistance was able to crawl a very short distance. And finally, he was able to stay in a standing position as long as he was holding on to dad for security. So although he didn't actually crawl or walk (or even stand unassisted) these were all great developmental steps. Paxton has been holding on to objects, such as balls, but he hasn't been quite sure what to do with them. Until today when a staff member had messed with him a little too much and he took the ball he had in his hand and chucked it at her face. Lol (I know I shouldn't laugh, they have all been great. But I did actually yell good throw. Oops). On the downside they do think his vision has been affected to some degree. The lady from rehab said that is very common unfortunately and that vision often takes 6-8 months to fully recover. Which might explain why he didn't recognize us at first and why he was/is REALLY scared a majority of the time, as well as having hard time tracking objects. Anyway, we will have to wait and see how that plays out. But patience is a virtue during this process so I won't panic yet. All and all he's still making progress. He's been cleared to be moved down to the rehab floor, we are just waiting for insurance to clear it and we're officially off the Neuro floor. I apologize to anyway that text today and I didn't respond. I had Pax all by myself today (Dez was spending some much needed time with the girls). But thank you so much for you texts and all of you for your support and continued prayers! ❤🙏
Like • Comment • Share • 65 Nancy B., Amber A. and 62 others •
Comments

Rob S.: Appetite like his dad, strong like his mom! Glad to hear that he's doing so great bro!
Like • Reply • July 13 at 8:30pm • Edited

Elizabeth D.: So glad he is enjoying food. that is a good sign!!! 🙏🙏🙏🙏💚💚
Like • Reply • July 13 at 8:30pm

Anne M.: Great update!
Like • Reply • July 13 at 8:33pm

Lisa W.: Thank you for the update! Was hoping things were progressing and some normalcy was happening. Keeping all of you in our thoughts and prayers. Sounds like he's doing great!
Like • Reply • July 13 at 8:44pm

Anissa C.: Lolol will then I would had thrown the ball to. Lolol it's good he's doing great
Like • Reply • July 13 at 8:49pm

Ana G.: This is great news Steven! I'm so happy to hear that he's got his appetite back! All our patients send there love & prayers to you baby boy & family! 😊😳😲❤️❤️💃
Like • Reply • July 13 at 9:01pm

Brian W.: Hey Dad, if I remember that's why they kept you in right field! You were no pitcher! Great day, again thanks for the update...
Like • Reply • July 13 at 9:13pm

Kim P.: God has brought Pax from death to life & he's not done with the miracles that are in store... He threw a ball at someone's face! Awesome! He ate like his dad likes to eat - Incredible! I can't wait to see what's next! You are one of the best, most precious dads I know and he is so lucky to have you yell "good throw!". You are a true witness of a good dad - a good man & your family is so

proud of you! Hang in there Dad! He's movin' & a shakin' & he'll be back before ya know it!
Like • Reply • 1 • July 14 at 12:25am

Stephanie Z.: I think being able to eat, sit, crawl, roll over, and stand with assistance is some pretty huge developments. From where he was to where he is now is great and amazing. I'm so happy for you guys. Thank you for the continuing updates.
Like • Reply • July 14 at 8:33am

Steve Riggs
July 14 at 8:45am • Phoenix, AZ •
Today I will be spending the day with my 2 amazing little girls! It's been a long time since they've been able to get Dads undivided attention and they deserve it. So I'm not sure what kind of updates I'll be able to give today. But already this morning Paxton was playing with toys, laughing and being silly. Dez and I both agreed this morning he definitely looked and sounded like "Paxton" which puts the biggest smile on my face. He also will NOT let us just hold him. He wants to be on the ground so he can try to walk. He's now going from his back, to his stomach, to all fours and then up on his legs if he's holding our hands. While on his legs he can kinda "squat" or "bounce". Walking is a work in progress. But he is DETERMINED to the point that he wears himself out. And this was just over night. I hate to get to excited, but the progress we are seeing is SO fast that it gives me hope that this will be a few/several month rehab instead of a couple year rehab. We'll see how his vision is, as well as a few other things that seem to be affected. But I'm absolutely blown away by his progress. Between the grace of God, the amazing medical staff, his own determination and all the support he continues to defy odds daily! Anyway, I'm off to enjoy two little beautiful blondies for the day. God bless you all and have a wonderful day! ❤️👼
Like • Comment • Share • 54 Loretta K., Kim P. and 51 others • Comments

Ana G.: Good Morning Steven! Great news from you about Paxton he's a fighter & is determined to what he needs to do!!That's great! #PraiseGod Enjoy your day with your babygirls you all deserve it!❤
Like • Reply • July 14 at 8:54am

Nancy B.: Great way to start my day. Thank you for the good news report. Give B and B a big hug from me.
Like • Reply • July 14 at 9:00am

Sheryl C.: It warms my heart to hear the wonderful news! Continued blessings for all of you!

Like • Reply • July 14 at 9:12am

Rach S.: That's so amazing. I Amani happy for him and you guys. Such a miracle he is and a blessing
Like • Reply • July 14 at 8:55pm

Steve Riggs
July 14 at 9:15am •
6 am... And getting better. Love the excited little fist pump at the end.

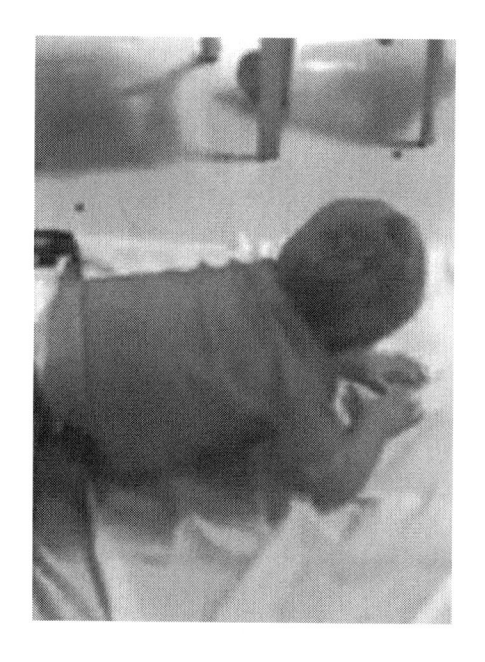

Comment • Share 54 Nancy B., Amber A. and 52 others 1 share •
Comments

Mike Meg K.: Beautiful sight!
Like • Reply • July 14 at 9:21am

Deana P.: Good job Paxton, so proud of you.
Like • Reply • July 14 at 9:27am

Jessica G.: Yay!!!!!
Like • Reply • July 14 at 9:30am

Amber A.: Such a strong little guy! So happy to see him up on his feet.
Like • Reply • July 14 at 10:22am

Amy H.: Love, love, love! Paxton, you are absolutely AMAZING!
Like • Reply • July 14 at 10:29am

Judy K.: Happy tears!
Like • Reply • July 14 at 12:21pm

Shelly S.: Yeah!!! He looks awesome and with his determination ... look out world!!! You GO Paxton!!! :)
Like • Reply • July 14 at 1:19pm

Loretta K.: Love love love it
Like • Reply • July 14 at 1:23pm

Dennis S. He is so adorable!!!!
Like • Reply • July 14 at 2:45pm

Sheryl C.: Yayyyy! Thank our most loving Creator! This beautiful boy will show us all.
Like • Reply • July 14 at 5:49pm

Rach S.: Awe that's so awesome. He's so cute
Like • Reply • July 14 at 8:51pm

Karin P.: Great!
Like • Reply • July 15 at 8:02am

Steve Riggs
July 14 at 9:05pm • Phoenix, AZ •
Day 11- I was gone for most of the day with the girls so there isn't too much to post. But Paxton did get transferred to the rehab floor (last step!) And he is an absolute crazy man!! He WON'T sit still. He wants down constantly and fusses and wiggles until you let him down. He wants to try to walk ALL DAY to the point he just wears himself out into a crying fussy mess. He still lacks the coordination to walk, so it's a workout just catching him and making sure he doesn't hurt himself. But man is he determined!!! They are making him sleep in a tent looking thing instead of a crib because they think he's a danger to himself in a crib. Anyway, he's now walking if he holds your hands. And although they are definitely awkward steps he is on both legs/feet, left, right, left, right so who cares. On to day 12. Let's see what this boy can do tomorrow! ❤️🙈
Like • Comment • Share • 55 Nancy B., Amber A. and 53 others •
Comments

Linda G.: thanks for the updates! they're appreciated because Paxton and your family are in my prayers, thoughts and heart always!! Keep up the great work little one!!
Like • Reply • July 14 at 9:11pm

Rach S.: I am so proud of you guys as parents. You guys are doing amazing.
Like • Reply • July 14 at 9:20pm

Alisha G.: Defying the odds. Love the updates.
Like • Reply • July 14 at 9:21pm

Richie R.: Amazing! Look forward to the updates every day. So glad he is continuing to do well. Tonight at dinner Maddie prayed for him to continue to get better!
Like • Reply • July 14 at 9:30pm

Travis K. Bri A.: Crazy man today!
Like • Reply • July 14 at 10:01pm

Desiree M.: Awesome! You'll be out of there in no time!
Like • Reply • July 15 at 7:17am

Anissa C.: They put him in jail, brake out lil man. Lol it sounds like he's going to be and do great things when he gets older. Good job lil man keep up the hard work. Your mom and dad needs the work out! Lol
Like • Reply • July 15 at 9:03am

Justin F.: Keep the great updates coming!!!
Like • Reply • July 15 at 1:23pm

Steve Riggs
July 15 at 12:21pm • Phoenix, AZ •
So tonight I'll give my true update. But right now I wanted to take just a second to thank a very special group of people I really haven't had a chance to thank yet. I want to thank all of you who donated to the gofund.com that Dez's sister set up for us. Between the $12,000 out of network max, rehab costs, prescription costs, not to mention the missed time at work I'm not sure what Dez and I would have done without you. It AMAZES me that between family, friends, friends OF friends and complete strangers, Sheena (Dez's sister) has been able to raise over $20,000 to help with our medical expenses. Over 150 people donated. And Paxton's story was shared over 1,500 TIMES on Facebook!!!!! Unbelievable. The amount of people that came out of the woodwork to help us warms my heart. I could NEVER express enough gratitude. So between my prayer warriors, supporters, family that came to help, and you people that contributed to this fund, you have made a horrible situation better. From the BOTTOM OF MY HEART thank you and God bless!❤️🙏

gofund.com
gofund.com
gofund.com
Like • Comment • Share • 34 Kim P., Diane M. and 31 others •
Comments

Steve T.: You and Dez are amazing people, true friends and spectacular parents. People value you guys and your family and we pray for the best sir!
Like • Reply • July 15 at 12:52pm

Dennis S.: I'm curious Steve - why is Paxton considered Out-of-Network at Phoenix Children's Hospital? There are only 2 children's hospitals that I know of, PCH being the main one for downtown and west-side and then Banner Desert in Mesa for the east-side. Since the accident occurred way out in NW Phoenix, is that why he was sent to PCH instead of Banner Desert or is PCH the children's

trauma center? It's just a curiosity question, if it's too involved don't worry. Since I tend to hit my out-of-pocket max every year myself, it's just one of those things I tend to pay attention to. But actually, if it's an emergency and life-threatening, I thought out-of-network didn't apply. Insurance is always so incredibly confusing. Did you get the Gilbert employee's PTO contribution yet? Hope that helps, too!
Like • Reply • July 15 at 1:27pm

Steve R.: About the PTO, Mary told me that several employees had donated PTO to help me out. So thank you guys so much. Keeping an income going while all this is going on is a huge weight lifted off my shoulders. So thank you again. About the out of network. I'm not sure. He is under Dez's insurance but it has to do with Banner and its relationship with Cardon's Children's Hospital since it's a banner hospital. And yes, the accident occurred at Dez's sister's house. That's why he was sent to PCH. Dez is pretty sure that if Cardon's had a pediatric rehab they may have even twisted our arm into transferring Pax over there to do the inpatient rehab. As far as the life threatening portion that's a question I don't have an answer to. Dez has been dealing with the insurance portion of it
Like • Reply • July 15 at 3:10pm

Dennis S.: Insurance is always a joy to work with - I know very well from my 2,357 surgeries I've had in the last few years!! I always love when your surgeon is in-network, the hospital is, you think you're all set - but the anesthesiologist is out-of-network - but of course, you don't know that until after the fact. That's so messed up. Thanks for answering, I know you have better things to do. I wasn't aware of the gofund.com account, very glad people are so generous. I'm still paying off my last $200k surgery (well, my $8k part) BUT amazingly I for once, when I'm NOT working, actually have PTO built up so I was able to help that way. You guys have a lot of people who love and care for all of you :-)
Like · Reply · July 15 at 3:31pm

Rach S.: Awe I am so glad God met your guys needs. Love this ;)

Like • Reply • July 15 at 5:57pm

Cathy V.: What is the gofund me called?
Like • Reply • July 15 at 6:02pm

Steve R.: Prayers for Pax-aroo. This isn't the link. Just the picture...

Like • Reply • 1 • July 15 at 6:33pm

Steve Riggs
July 15 at 8:32pm • Gilbert, AZ •
Day 12: The good news, Paxton is tube, wire, cord, needle-free after getting his feeding tube removed today. Bad news is he kinda had a rough day. Physical therapy and occupational therapy were both a challenge. I think he was just physically and emotionally exhausted, so he fussed and cried most of the day☹ and with brain injuries it's so tough to tell whether it's the injury causing the emotion, the meds, frustration, fatigue or sadness. But either way it's tough to see your boy have a tough day. But by the end of the night he was doing much better and we had our first family meal together outside of Paxton's hospital room. Which he acted like a crazy man, ripped his chicken noodle soup out of my hand and poured it all the way down the front of himself. Which was "so Paxton". Lol. But regardless if he had a rough day or not I'm very proud of how hard he has fought. He's still doing well, making slow and steady progress. Hoping for big things tomorrow for him!!! And hoping he wakes up with that handsome little smile of his on his face. Until tomorrow, have a good night everyone. ❤🙈
Like • Comment • Share • 43 Nancy B., Amber A. and 41 others 1 share • Comments

Brian W.: That is oddly familiar behavior from a time long long ago in a place far away! From the peanut gallery, they all seem like fabulously bitchin' days!! :)
Like • Reply • July 15 at 8:36pm

Rach S..: He is doing so amazing. It's totally a God thing and Paxton's strong will ;)
Like • Reply • July 15 at 8:49pm

Linda G.: happy you had a family time!! it's good for all of you!! in prayers always ❤
Like • Reply • July 15 at 9:09pm

Stephanie Z.: He is one strong little boy
Like • Reply • July 15 at 9:11pm

Anne M.: Slow and steady wins the race.
Like • Reply • 1 • July 15 at 9:14pm

Ana G.: This is great news Steven! I'm sorry he had a rough day but it's not always gona be good! One day at a time! Hugs and kisses to the baby boy!! 😮❤️❤️
Like • Reply • July 15 at 9:21pm

Steve Riggs
July 16 at 7:25am • Gilbert, AZ •
Breakfast time on the Rehab floor. Served with a smile. ❤🫂

Like • Comment • Share • 69 Loretta K., Amber A. and 66 others 1 share • Comments

Donna B.: precious
Like • Reply • July 16 at 8:03am

Stephanie Z.: OMG he looks so good 😊
Like • Reply • July 16 at 8:07am

Ana G.: Amazing! Good Morning Baby boy Paxton! #Godisgood #Powerofprayer 😊👶❤️❤️👣
Like • Reply • July 16 at 8:41am

Mike Meg K.: Lookin' good little man!
Like • Reply • July 16 at 9:11am

Steve R.: Milestone of the day. I know it may not seem like a big deal, but being able to pick up a small object(fruit loop) and bring it to his mouth are both firsts since his accident. Previously he couldn't even locate small objects let alone pick them up and have that connection of hand to mouth. With God's grace and his determination... This boys not done yet!
 Like • Reply • 16 • July 16 at 9:21am

Rach S.: That is so awesome
Like • Reply • July 16 at 9:48am

Sheryl C.: Beautiful, just Beautiful!!!
Like • Reply • July 16 at 11:08am

Brad J.: This is so great!
Like • Reply • July 16 at 9:48am

Rach S.: Blows me away to see his progress. He is so cute
Like • Reply • July 16 at 9:48am

Judy K.: He looks so good...strong boy...thank you God!
Like • Reply • July 16 at 10:01am

 Loretta K.: Very strong boy.. God is good
Like · Reply · July 16 at 1:10pm

Cassie M.: This is so awesome! What a miracle! Thank you for sharing and keeping us all updated. So proud of him ❤
Like • Reply • July 16 at 10:22am

Lisa M.: Such a cutie! 🖤 Thanks for sharing! So amazing Prayers and hugs!!
Like • Reply • July 16 at 11:16am

Steve Riggs
July 16 at 9:30pm • Phoenix, AZ •
Day 13: In 2 days (Monday) it will be the 2 week anniversary of Paxton's accident. People might think I'm over exaggerating when I talk about his condition when he was found. That he may have stop breathing for a second or that his heart was immediately restarted. According to a family member that was there at the time, Paxton was grey when he was found. His lips and eyelids were purple. He had no pulse and no heartbeat. When admitted into the ER they look at several things to give us an early indication on his prognosis. His bodies PH, which was horrible. His blood gases (CO_2 levels), horrible as well. And finally his CT scan, which they showed us. There is supposed to be a separation between the white and grey matter in his brain with distinct lines and distance between his brain and the skull. I can personally attest that it was one big white blob with no distance between the brain and the skull to allow for additional swelling (keep in mind the brain continues to swell for 72 hours). He was placed in a sedated coma and placed on a cooling blanket (essentially on ice) because his body was on fire (fever) from the trauma. At that point they said he would die or possibly be in a vegetative state for the rest of his life. Or as the Dr put it, it was certain that he would have severe brain damage. As he survived day 1... Day 2.... Day 3... It became apparent he would live. Then he faced Nuero Storming. Then seizures. The Drs said he faced an EXTENSIVE rehabilitation ahead that could last years. On Day 9 Pax was released from the Pediatric ICU. Day 11 he was discharged from the Neuro floor. This morning he ate on his own. By this afternoon he was walking. I'm not talking 1-2 steps. I'm talking 15-20 steps. Were they a little awkward? Maybe. But not bad considering the docs said to expect 3 days to recover for every 1 day in bed. I believe that would be around 30 days? He did it in 3. 2 days ago they said he had vision issues that could take 6-8 months to return. Today he was picking up fruit loops off his high chair. There are some things that medical science can't explain. And although I've never been a truly religious man, I know what I have seen, what I believe, and what I felt. And if you read the medical facts, this was not supposed to turn out this way. But it

did. I will be forever grateful for that. And I will also forever be amazed at the determination and fight in my boy as well. The frustration he showed when he couldn't do something he wanted to. The drive and persistence to try until he could. I'm not sure if I could have done the things he did. I've never been so proud. Anyway, it's not over yet. There are still hurdles to overcome. But I have NO DOUBT this will be a story of full recovery. A true miracle derived from faith and determination. Thank you all again for your prayers (and for reading my ramblings, again. Lol). God bless and have a wonderful day tomorrow. ❤️🙏

Like • Comment • Share • 57 Amber A., Kim P. and 55 others 11 shares • Comments

Brian W.: Wow, amazing everytime I think about it. One of those feel good stories of my long life time! So happy for you and your family, and especially Pax...Guess I finally have to admit that miracles do happen!
Like • Reply • 1 • July 16 at 9:39pm

Shannon D.: Absolutely amazing! He has amazing parents who are strong, beautiful sisters who love beyond measure and tons of family and friends praying for him. So happy to hear the wonderful report!! 👆🙌
Like • Reply • July 16 at 9:43pm

Rob S.: By the grace of God brother!
Like • Reply • July 16 at 9:45pm

Rach S.: Wow, this is incredible. Your guys faith has been amazing. I am just blown away at this. Not everyday we get to see a miracle like this. Every time I read your updates, I get chills. Thank you lord for saving Pax and giving him another chance at life. Thank you lord for giving his parents another chance to hold their baby boy. I am so happy for you guys and as always will continue to pray🙏😊🙌
Like • Reply • 1 • July 16 at 9:57pm

Amy H.: Miracle boy! 🖤
Like • Reply • July 16 at 10:06pm

Lauren F.: Truly amazing! Your boy is definitely meant to be here! Way to go little guy!
Like • Reply • July 16 at 10:08pm

Jenna S.: It truly blows my mind how far he has come in such a short amount of time. I think it's hard for people who haven't seen him in person or how he was those first few days to really grasp how awesome and miraculous his progress has been.
Like • Reply • 1 • July 16 at 10:18pm

Elizabeth D.: Wonderful news, he is meant to be here for great things. God bless, prayers ongoing. 🙏🙏🙏🖤
Like • Reply • July 16 at 10:22pm

Jessica G.: Paxton & your families journey has made me take a close look at my faith. I've prayed harder than I have in years. And today donated blood for the first time to help hopefully another family in need. These updates are so appreciated. And so thankful that Paxton has his father's fighting spirit!!!!
Like • Reply • 2 • July 16 at 10:35pm

Kerri C.: God is great and He has plans for that special boy.
Like • Reply • July 16 at 11:07pm

Steve T.: Couldn't be happier!!!
Like • Reply • July 16 at 11:17pm

Linda G.: have always thought of you as one of "my boys" and so good to know your son is so much like you!! always in my heart and prayers!! keep on one day at a time and one step at a time!! Paxton can and will...🖤
Like • Reply • 2 • July 17 at 12:01am • Edited

Meagan S.: I have always had a special place in my heart for Jon, Steve and Robert, too. :)
Like • Reply • 1 • July 17 at 12:06am

Meagan S.: Steve, this is such incredible news. I'm so happy for you all. Your family's love and strength is indescribable. Keep it up!
Like • Reply • July 17 at 12:10am

Adam Elizabeth G.: Love the posts! They are worth saving to read over years from now when Pax is older!
Like • Reply • July 17 at 12:32am

Donna B.: God is so good!!
Like • Reply • July 17 at 7:01am

Monika G.: God blessed that boy 🙂
Like • Reply • July 17 at 7:35am

Travis K. Bri A.: Amen!! God is great!! 🙏
Like • Reply • July 17 at 7:37am

Loretta K.: I love how you ramble.. it is for sure a Miracle.. place the credit where credit is due.. amen
Like • Reply • July 17 at 9:09am

Shelly S.: Steve, God does miracles and without a doubt Paxton is one of them! I continue to pray for all of you, especially Paxton! May your story show others God's never ending love!!😄💖🙏
Like • Reply • July 17 at 9:37am

Anissa C.: Amen to that! I've been praying my butt off! As well as everyone one else. I'm so happy and proud of lil man . And my boy Steve you would had made it through to because you have Dez and those beautiful kids! So yes you would had been just as strong and determined as Paxton. I have nothing but love for my extended family! 🙂
Like • Reply • July 17 at 9:58am • Edited

Diane M.: Hey Steve, if you write the book about Paxton's miracle I will surely read it!!!!
Like • Reply • July 17 at 6:57pm

Steve Riggs
July 17 at 8:20pm • Gilbert, AZ •

Every night I write about Paxton's health. The progress he's made, and the milestones he's reached. The number of steps that he's taken, or the thing he's physically able to do. I'm not going to do that tonight. Did he hit a couple milestones? Yes. But I'd rather talk about something else he's been able to do. He's able to hold up his arms because he wants his dad to hold him. And when I pick him up he sometimes even leans his head on my shoulder to give me a hug. If I say "kisses?" And smack my lips, he smacks his lips back at me before I kiss him. He high fives me. And I've reminded him how to "honk my nose". And he smiles and giggles at me every time I make the honking noise. This afternoon at nap time he was fussy in his tent thing where he sleeps. So I squeezed in, he laid his head on my chest and I rubbed his back until he fell asleep. We napped together for two hours. I almost never got to feel his warmth on my chest ever again. See I get caught up on milestones sometimes because I want my boy to live a normal healthy life growing up. I don't want him to have any limitations. But I forget to post about the most important things. The things that only a dad feels with his boy. The love, the laughter, the smiles, the bond. These are the things that make me happiest during his recovery. The fact that I get to tell him "I love you" and get a smile when we're being goofy. Those are the things I most thankful for. So I'm taking a night off from posting about milestones. And just want to post about how lucky I am to have my same wonderful, silly, loving little man back. More naps together. More high fives. More hugs and more kisses. And even more honking Dad's nose. ❤️👶

Like • Comment • Share • 60 Nancy B., Amber A. and 58 others •
Comments

Richie Nikki R.: Melts my heart, so glad he is doing so well!
Like • Reply • 1 • July 17 at 8:26pm

Steve T.: Thanks for letting us visit tonight! It was great to see you and the whole family. PAXTON sure has a way of putting a smile on all our faces! And He is lucky to have wonderful amazing parents like you and Dez! So so so happy brother!
Like • Reply • 1 • July 17 at 8:27pm

Alisha G.: This is my favorite update. Just a dad. And his boy. And the little things. I'm so happy you get to honk noses.
Like • Reply • 4 • July 17 at 8:41pm

Cathy V.: I'm so happy for you and your family!!! Keep up the good work Paxton!!
Like • Reply • 1 • July 17 at 9:39pm

Rob S.: In tears over here bro. So damn happy for y'all!
Like • Reply • 1 • July 17 at 10:26pm

Rach S.: That's the best. Sometimes we can take the little things in life for granted, awesome to see you taking every moment in. Thanks for sharing this!
Like • Reply • 1 • July 17 at 10:31pm

Anissa C.: Ok tears lots of tears, so glad he's doing great.
Like • Reply • 1 • July 18 at 10:40am

Steve Riggs
July 18 at 9:06pm • Phoenix, AZ •

2 week anniversary of Paxton's accident: Although Pax did well today in rehab it was kind of bittersweet. After Dez answered questions with the Dr and rehab specialist, they determined cognitively he is currently that of a 6 month old and expressively that of a 9 month old. I had 2 thoughts. My initial thought was that shocks me. And it made me a little sad. He doesn't seem that different to me than before the accident. But then again I'm a proud dad. And maybe I forget certain things he used to do before the accident like open doors, flip through books, or run to the bathroom when I tell him it's time to brush his teeth or take a bath. Also it's been a while since he was 9 months so I guess I forget how "expressive" a 9 month old is. But my second thought was, after all this who cares if he's behind 9 months. Or even a year. He just went from basically no brain activity to 9 months in 10 days. And it's not like he can't catch up with a little hard work. And let's face it, it could have and SHOULD have been much worse. With his knack for beating the odds, something tells me he'll probably grow up to be a brain surgeon or something anyway. But COMPLETELY changing the subject, you know what you never too old for? Stomping in mud puddles. And that's what I got to do with Pax after it rained tonight. Out there in the rehab playground in his pajamas and bare feet stomping away getting soaking wet. I'm sure the medical staff probably thought I was insane. But I couldn't pass up a chance to do something that would make us laugh together. I guess if there is a silver lining to all this it's that. Tomorrow isn't guaranteed. Laugh and smile at every chance you get. Things can change in an instant. ❤🙈

Like • Comment • Share 54 • Katie R., Nancy B. and 52 others •
Comments

Brian W.: Not trying to be trite or funny, but I am told regulary by a certain woman that I am about a 9 month old! Plus at my age I'm closer to being in diapers then Pax is to be out of them! As a friend, I see being able to quantify where your little man is, as a sort of victory, you might not realize it now, but it's somewhere to start.

Like • Reply • 1 • July 18 at 9:15pm

Rob S.: Not trying to point out the elephant in the room bro, but Pax died. Not like a second or two, but like dead dead. I've held dead babies and dead bodies before, and it's hard to describe that once the soul leaves there is a nothingness to them.

As a Christian man, I know that when we die, our soul is with God for judgement in an instant. Not a second or a minute, but in an instant. For someone Pax's age, there is no doubt that he would have gone to heaven.

Anyways bro, your son DIED. In an instant his soul is in heaven with God. For some reason, be it for his good, for your good, or for the world's good, God decided that he had some more time in store for Paxton..... and thus, he sent Paxton back.

Miracles aren't always easy & there usually isn't a very good testimony without a tragedy. God put Pax on earth for a reason, and then God sent him back for a reason. I'm pretty sure that the 9 months that Paxton is "behind" is accounted for in the big picture somewhere bro. Just gotta have faith & celebrate the wins!
Like • Reply • 3 • July 18 at 9:38pm

Rob S.: Plus, what the hell do doctors know? They thought I might not be able to walk again! God's in control bro!
Like • Reply • July 18 at 9:39pm

Jessica G.: Love this "big brother". Stomping in mud puddles is what boys are best at!!! Paxton is so lucky to have such awesome parents, sisters, etc to help remind him who he is and help him to grow.
Like • Reply • 2 • July 18 at 10:44pm

Alisha G.: Sounds like a lesson in enjoying. And celebrating. The little things. And when you think about that. What a gift. We should all be doing this. But we get busy. Or distracted. And you're

right. Tomorrow is no guarantee. So go stomp in puddles. Today.
....You are sharing a precious gift...thank you for that. ❤️🙏
Like • Reply • 3 • July 19 at 1:02am

Steve Riggs
July 19 at 10:37am • Phoenix, AZ •

Sooo... I just had a meeting with what seemed like half the hospital. lol. By Thursday Pax will be down to 1 medication (the seizure medication as a precautionary med). By Friday they will remove him from his tent/jail and get him back in a crib. And next Tuesday they plan to SEND HIM HOME! 🙏🙏🙏 He will still need 3 hours of outpatient rehab a day. So any normalcy is a ways away. But getting him home to familiar surroundings will do everyone's heart good! ❤️🐵

Like • Comment • Share 55 • Nancy B., Amber A. and 52 others •
Comments

Deana P.: That's great news
Like • Reply • July 19 at 10:41am

Desiree M.: Happy happy joy Joy! So great to hear that 😀
Like • Reply • July 19 at 10:42am

Shelly S.: That's awesome!!! I'm guessing HOME will be wonderful medicine for him ... AND the whole family!!! God Bless and prayers are continuing!!! =D
Like • Reply • July 19 at 10:42am

Brad J.: Truly wonderful news... thanks for all the updates. You are all always on my mind. Wishing him the very best.
Like • Reply • July 19 at 10:44am

Steve T.: Amazing 👍 👍
Like • Reply • July 19 at 10:54am

Ana G.: That's good news Steven! #PraiseGod Way to God Paxton & Thank you to all the Dr's & Nurses at PCH!!😊❤️❤️❤️
Like • Reply • July 19 at 10:57am

Judy K.: Best news ever!
Like • Reply • July 19 at 10:57am:

Rach S.: This is the best news. Yay Go PAX GO!! So happy for you guys. He is a tuff cookie ;)
Like • Reply • July 19 at 11:28am

Stephanie Z.: That is such good news!!! It will do him good to be back home 😁
Like • Reply • July 19 at 11:33am

Shannon D.: That's amazing news!!
Like • Reply • July 19 at 11:41am

Brian W.: Home=good!
Like • Reply • July 19 at 11:44am

Lisa W.: Home has got to be better! And hours with his sisters will be better than rehab, right? So happy for all of you!
Like • Reply • July 19 at 11:48am

Adam Elizabeth G.: So so so amazing God is good!!!!!!!
Like • Reply • July 19 at 12:31pm

Adam Elizabeth G.: A very minor, minor story in comparison to what Pax is going thru but Caleb had a minor surgery when he was 3 and REALLY reacted bad to the anesthesia!! He was confused and disoriented which is normal, at first, but would not open his eyes and just Screamed Screamed and Screamed!!!!! It was horrifying to watch, I (Liz) held him, talked to him ....nothing could calm him down not even time....finally they just released him like that (I think he was freaking out the other patients in the outpatient recovery area) he did that constant scream all the way out of the hospital, the whole car ride and into the house. I got him settled in and life went on in our house and in a few min he instantly stopped and asked for a popsicle?!?! Such a creepy thing but being home and being a part of normal family life is the best way (when medically stable of course) to recover!! Especially when your younger sister is like "stop screaming jeezzz!!!" Lol
Like • Reply • 2 • July 19 at 12:44pm

Rob S.: For all of Steve and Deserae's friends & family, we have made a page for them on Take Them A Meal. We are hoping to get enough people to sign up so that they won't have to worry about dinners for the first week. Please see the link provided on Steve's FB and sign up if you are able to, but no worries if you can't! Thanks & God bless.
Like • Reply • 1 • July 19 at 1:33pm

Deana P.: I don't see the link
Like • Reply • July 19 at 1:35pm

Deana Parra.: Thanks
Like • Reply • July 19 at 1:36pm

Rob S.: First link was the admin link 🙂

http://www.takethemameal.com/meals.php?t=YNZG3182

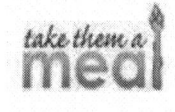

take them a meal

Meals For . . . Paxton Riggs
Click on the link above to view the meal schedule for Paxton Riggs on TakeThemAMeal.com.
takethemameal.com
Like • Reply • 1 • July 19 at 1:46pm

Noelle G.: God is good!!!! I can't express how happy we are for Pax, you and your family Steve. We will continue to keep everyone in our prayers
Like • Reply • July 19 at 2:46pm

Steve Riggs
July 20 at 9:54am •
Secretly he's training for the 2030 Olympics. Equipped with compression pants and stability harness. #olympicsorbust

Like • Comment • Share • 68 Loretta K., Amber A. and 65 others 1 share • Comments

Rob S.: Killin it!
Like • Reply • 1 • July 20 at 10:04am

Lisa W.: Man on a mission, for sure!
Like • Reply • July 20 at 10:15am

Travis K. Bri A.: Love this!! Such determination
Like • Reply • 1 • July 20 at 10:25am

Rach S.: Such a cute kid
Like • Reply • July 20 at 10:45am

Amy H.: Go get 'em Paxton! 😆
Like • Reply • July 20 at 11:05am

Sheryl C.: What an amazing little boy! And he is blessed with such loving and dedicated parents. ☺️🎶🌸💖
Like • Reply • July 20 at 11:24am

Dave M.: What a stud! Keep it up Pax!
Like • Reply • July 20 at 1:38pm

Anissa C.: Hahaha that's what Kendra was saying, a full day's ago.
Like • Reply • July 20 at 4:23pm

Steve Riggs
July 20 at 8:59pm • Phoenix, AZ •

Day 16... I think... All my days and nights are now starting to blend together. Anyway, two days ago when talking about the cognitive and expressive age level of Pax and I mentioned that he still hasn't done certain things he used to like flip through books, open doors, or run to the bathroom when I say "time to take a bath". Tonight he flipped through a book, tried to open doors (they have codes), and although he wasn't running he does light up when I say trigger words like "bath" or "outside". I think God actually reads my Facebook posts (I'm sure he has nothing better to do right?) and thinks, "Seriously? Is he really complaining that Paxton isn't able to do THAT now!?", shakes his head at me, and then boom within a couple days he's able to do it. Lol. Ok, probably not, but he did do much better on his fine motor skills today. For example he was able to play with toys that involved pressing small buttons, he's picking up small objects up with much more ease, as well as showing significant improvement at simple cognitive toys such as putting the plastic rings over/onto the little plastic pole. I will say at times I'm often curious about the therapist methodologies, but I will fully admit that his progress still blows me away, so they obviously are very good at what they do. I'm very grateful for everything the medical staff here at PCH has done!! They have been nothing short of amazing. Anyway, tonight Pax was moved to a crib instead of his tent thingy so we'll see how that goes. Wish me luck. But it's just one more step towards releasing him to the wild. And that can't come soon enough! Until tomorrow take care everyone and again thank you for the love, prayers and support! ❤️🙏

Like • Comment • Share 50 Amber A., Kim P. and 47 others •
Comments

Dennis S.: Steve are you or Dez staying with him all night (I would guess a children's hospital has beds in the room for a parent) so he's always got a familiar face to see if he's scared or just awake? Hope you're both getting enough rest. How are your girls doing through all of this? I could see how they could very easily get jealous of the time Pax takes from them. Anyway, I'm so glad to

hear he's doing so well and I bet you're counting the days to go home!
Like • Reply • 1 • July 20 at 9:08pm

Steve R.: We were staying every night until he got moved to rehab. But on the rehab floor only one parent can stay the night. So we are alternating 1 on, 1 off, 1 on, etc. It's a lot of driving but each kid gets ample time with both parents that way.
Like • Reply • 3 • July 20 at 9:11pm

Cassie M.: Amazing! One determined kid ❤
Like • Reply • July 20 at 9:54pm

Myra A.-R.: All of your updates make my heart smile ☺❤ We are rooting for Paxton and are continuing to pray for his speedy recovery. 🙏 I am in awe of his resilience and the miracle of God's healing hands. He's such a tough little guy. 💪 Big hugs ~ The Ruperto family
Like • Reply • July 20 at 9:54pm

Rach S.: Yay PAX. Love the part where you talk about God shaking his head lol. Sometimes that happens in my personal life and I wonder the same ;).
Like • Reply • July 21 at 6:14am

Anissa C.: Go lil man. High Five Paxton!
Like • Reply • July 21 at 6:45am

Steve Riggs
July 21 at 9:52pm • Gilbert, AZ •

The 4th of July was the night of Paxton's accident. I still get a little choked up when I go back and read the first few posts that I wrote. It's almost surreal to see the pictures. To see Paxton in a coma, wires and tubes coming from everywhere while my girls sang itsy bitsy spider to him. I can still hear his heartbreaking distorted cry when they removed his ventilator tube and started bringing him out of sedation. The body stiffening and moans during the Neuro storming. The lifeless look in his eyes and repetitive body motions during his seizures. Watching someone else's blood being put into my son when his blood cells dropped significantly and they couldn't tell why. But then progress started to happen. Then progress turned into a miracle. Paxton started defying the odds and time tables they set for him day after day after day. You start to smile and laugh. You're proud and joyful until you almost forget about the pain of the first several days. Tomorrow will be 2 weeks and 4 days since the accident. How many of you have had colds last longer than that? Or sprained an ankle that still hurt 3 weeks after the injury. I only mention this because Pax was scheduled to be discharged on Tuesday. Today he showed up at therapy and once again baffled them with the progress he made in just ONE DAY. It was so much progress that the Rehab Doc couldn't justify keeping him any longer. So it's only fitting that Pax beat one last deadline. One last time frame. Tomorrow he will be released to go home to his family. Home to his own bed, his own toys, his own crazy sisters and both his loving parents. Home to where he can grunt and point and that back door when he wants to go outside. Home to where he can sit in his high chair and eat dinner with his family....... And then throw food on the floor and look at us with a devious smile to signal that he's done. This was a very bittersweet experience for me. It was without a doubt the worst 2 weeks of my life. But it taught me a lot about faith. A lot about the power of prayer. It restored my faith in humanity. The strength of a family to come together when times are tough. It showed me that some of my friends, really are family to me. And when you're down, sometimes the people you least expect to be there are the first ones by your

side. It made me cherish every second I have with my kids. And it made me respect and love my wife more than I ever had before. It's funny when you hear someone say everything happens for a reason. Or that God has a plan, you just don't know what it is yet. You never truly understand it until something like this happens. I would NEVER wish this upon anyone. And I would never want my boy to have to experience that pain again. But I find solace in the things I've learned. You all have been such a huge part of this journey. And although Pax is closing in on the end of this chapter he still has rehab scheduled cleeeaarr through October. Lol. So I will continue to occasionally keep you posted. Thank you for being my support. My therapists. And my prayer groups. Miracles can happen. God bless and have a wonderful night❤️🙏
Like • Comment • Share 55 Katie R., Amber A. and 53 others •
Comments

Desiree M.: Very well said! I am grateful for this happy ending, thanks for taking the time to share this, much love 💜 to you and your family!
P.S. I think he might be an X-men?
Like • Reply • 1 • July 21 at 10:01pm • Edited

Shelly S.: That's the BEST news yet! Praise the Lord! Prayers will continue that progress continues and healing is quick! Love you guys!!!
Like • Reply • 1 • July 21 at 9:58pm

Sheryl C.: We are overjoyed with this news. Happy tears and thankful prayers. We ALL have been blessed. Blessed to witness miracles, faith in action, and the results of love from many people who have been watching this frightening event unfold. We are still here for you. Yayyyy Paxton!!!
Like • Reply • 4 • July 21 at 9:59pm

Brian W.: Wonderful news, after a few weeks of wonderful news! Thanks Steve for the updates, FB and your posts have allowed many people from your old Spokane days to be part of the silent support group. So happy.......
Like • Reply • 1 • July 21 at 10:04pm

Rob S.: So damn happy for you guys, and so thankful for what God has given you back brother. Stoked to see Paxton coming home!
Like • Reply • 3 • July 21 at 10:15pm

Rob S.: PS, still bringing meal over Tuesday, it's just what we do! Hope y'all have the greatest weekend ever this weekend!
Like • Reply • 3 • July 21 at 10:15pm

Steve R.: We look forward to it! The girls start school this week so it'll be a little crazy, so we're looking forward to it and seeing you guys again!!
Like · Reply · 2 · July 21 at 10:19pm

Rach S.: Everyday I started looking forward to your posts and anxiously waiting to see what's going on with Pax. Every post I read, my eyes would tear up with emotion. This is the best news. Thanks for keeping us in this journey with you. Continued prayers. Love you guys!
Like • Reply • 4 • July 21 at 10:18pm

Linda G.: remember you and family are in my heart, thoughts and prayers always!! appreciate your updates and please keep us posted as he comes home to your loving family! ❤
Like • Reply • 1 • July 21 at 10:25pm

Jenna S.: And you laughed at my 1 to 2 weeks comment!! Lol.
Like • Reply • July 21 at 10:44pm

Steve R.: Every time I talked to a Dr I hear about these goals. And to be patient. About how long this process will be. And then Pax blows those time lines away. I should probably stop doubting Pax. Lol
Like • Reply • July 22 at 6:47am

Stephanie Z.: I'm so happy he will be home soon right where he belongs with his family. What a strong little boy. He is proving to everyone that miracles do happen ❤
Like • Reply • 1 • July 21 at 11:25pm

Meagan S.: Steve, I am so happy for you all. This has been such an emotional experience. I'm so glad you shared it with us. Thank you for letting us help in our own ways - be it through physical presence or prayers or sending love across miles. Keep working. Keep loving. And please keep us updated when you can. Can't wait to see how fast he goes once he's home!
Like • Reply • 2 • July 21 at 11:45pm

Mary S.: Thanks so much for keeping us updated through your posts. It's such a relief to read about Pax's progress every day. I am so thankful for the positive outcome. I will never forget hearing the broken hearted tone to my sister's voice as she called to tell me the news of the accident. We held each other up over the phone and cried together, knowing the only thing left was prayer. Pray we did and this is one story to write down in the book of Answered Prayers! Love you guys and still praying for 100% recovery for Paxton.
Like • Reply • 2 • July 22 at 3:11am

Elizabeth D.: I am so happy for you and your family Steve. Keep us posted on his progress, he is a very special little boy! God bless 🙏🙏🙏❤
Like • Reply • 1 • July 22 at 7:17am

Shelly S.: Steve, you have been an excellent writer and have done an amazing job in keeping us updated and on top of how Paxton is doing. It has been very much appreciated and has helped us know how to pray! I am thrilled that you all get to be home together again! If you don't mind, please continue to keep us updated on progress, challenges, and specific prayer requests. I know there will be adjustments on everyone's behalf as you all try to get readjusted to being together - and hopefully back to some normalcy. We will continue to pray for everyone and know you are loved by us and the Lord Jesus!! After all he gave Paxton back to you!!!
Like • Reply • 1 • July 22 at 8:51am

Rose A.: Such a miracle!! I cannot begin to imagine what you all went through. Grateful for all the healers we can't see working miracles, so happy for You and your family! What a sweet little man!
Like • Reply • 1 • July 28 at 7:43pm

Steve Riggs
July 22 at 1:57pm • Phoenix, AZ •
And we're OUT!! ✌ Thanks for everything PCH!

Like • Comment • Share 72 Amber A., Kim P. and 70 others •
Comments

Deana P.: So happy for all of you.
Like • Reply • July 22 at 1:59pm

Ana G.: Yay!!How exciting!! Good luck Riggs Family!
#Homebound!!😊 ✌ ❤❤
Like • Reply • July 22 at 2:02pm

Steve T.: AMAZING!! SUPER PAXTON!!
Like • Reply • July 22 at 2:10pm

Stephanie Z.: Yay!!!!!🎉🎉🎉
Like • Reply • July 22 at 2:11pm

Justin F.: Huge shout out to the Riggs Family! So happy for you all ❤
Like • Reply • July 22 at 2:15pm

Noelle G.: God bless you all!! Miracles truly happen. Pax, you are an amazing inspiration to all of us!!! Bless you sweet baby boy
Like • Reply • July 22 at 2:18pm

Brad J.: Fantastic!
Like • Reply • July 22 at 2:21pm

Jami G.: Wonderful news!
Like • Reply • July 22 at 2:21pm

Kerri C.: Woot woot!!!!!!! So so overjoyed
Like • Reply • July 22 at 2:25pm

Rob S.: Only thing better than this picture of Pax coming home is God bringing him back. Welcome home little buddy!
Like • Reply • July 22 at 2:35pm

Jenna S.: YAAAAASSSSSSSS!
Like • Reply • July 22 at 2:36pm

Mike Meg K.: Awesome!!!!
Like • Reply • July 22 at 2:46pm

Rach S.: Good looking family. So exciting. 🖐📱😊🙆✋
Like • Reply • July 22 at 2:54pm

Alisha G.: Yay!! Many blessings for your weekend!! Enjoy!
Like • Reply • July 22 at 3:07pm

Judy K.: THANK YOU GOD! Amazing!
Like • Reply • July 22 at 4:08pm

Braidon F.: Yeah!!!!!
Like • Reply • July 22 at 6:51pm

Meagan S.: And how many seconds has Pax had not being loved on by his adorable sisters since you got discharged?!? :)
Like • Reply • July 22 at 7:24pm

Brian W.: Excellent, great day, with many many more ahead!
Like • Reply • July 22 at 8:08pm

Nancy B.: Now that's a great family photo!!!!
Like • Reply • July 22 at 8:32pm

Dennis S.: FANTASTIC!!!! I'm SO happy for you all, it's going to be just great to feel that your family is "complete" again. I'm sure that every single one of you are ecstatic on the way home. Steve, I'm so incredibly thrilled for ALL of you, I'm sure you'll all feel better very soon! Wonderful, wonderful, WONDERFUL!!!!
Like • Reply • July 23 at 1:23pm

Elizabeth D.: Fantastic!!!!
Like • Reply • July 23 at 3:48pm

EPILOGUE

Immediately after Paxton's accident, the outside world abruptly disappeared from the minds of those people who watched over Paxton in his hospital room. Thoughts that normally occupy minds were no longer important. Thoughts of world events, houses, cars, bank accounts, appearances, to-do lists, all thoughts except those thoughts of Paxton did not exist in their minds.

Within Paxton's room, the atmosphere of sadness and concern was heavy in the room. All eyes were on Paxton. And, all eyes were on the medical equipment which were monitoring Paxton's condition. Everyone in the room looked at the monitors in hope of seeing positive readings and in fear of seeing negative readings. There was a camera at the end of Paxton's bed so the neurologists could view him from outside the room by video.

Within Paxton's room, as the days went by, the atmosphere began to change. The air was still thick with sadness and concern but small, positive changes in Paxton's condition began to take place. And, the people inside Paxton's room could feel a seed of hope intensifying. Those who had spent days standing and sitting as they quietly watched over Paxton were becoming more active and vocal. There was the sound of surprise when a sedated Paxton first smiled. There was the vision of smiles on the faces of all the people in the room when Paxton would open his eyes and look around. There was the exclamation of happiness when Paxton would move his arms and legs. There was the sound of relief, joy and happy tears when the MRI came back with the result of no severe brain damage. There was the wide-eyed look of excitement when Paxton threw a ball. And, then, there were cheers of "Yay, Paxton!" and clapping as Paxton reached milestone after milestone.

Within Paxton's room, the doctor's announced that Paxton was ready to be moved out of ICU. There was joy and excitement that Paxton was well enough to take the next step toward being released from the hospital. Paxton left his hospital room in the ICU for a hospital room on a lower floor. And, within that room, there was the happy shock of disbelief on faces when Paxton rolled over and got onto his hands and knees. Two days later, Paxton was moved to a third room which was in the rehabilitation wing of the hospital. Within that room, there was celebration when Paxton began to walk. The weariness of watching over the still boy in the hospital bed was replaced by the exhaustion of constantly trying to keep up with an active young boy who didn't want to stop moving. Paxton was allowed to leave his room. Now, there were happy family meals together sitting around a large table in the hospital cafeteria. Paxton, in his high chair, was the center of attention. But now, all around Paxton were observing him with smiles and laughter.

    Within Paxton's room, on their final day at the hospital, the family packed up their belongings to go home with their baby boy. They were filled with joy to know their family would all be together again within their home. And, their son would be able to sleep in his very own bed within Paxton's room.

UPDATE

Steve Riggs
August 23 • Gilbert •
The aftermath: Most of the time you hear the term aftermath it is used as negative term. It is defined as "the period of time after a bad, usually destructive event". But I guess it depends on what you do with that period of time after the "event" that makes it good or bad. In our case, the "aftermath" isn't bad. As a matter of fact it's amazing. We are blessed with what is left over, and we cherish it daily. For an entire month I was very candid with you all. So it's only fitting that in what might be my last IN DEPTH "Paxton update" I'm just the same. So this is our aftermath of July 4th. Since we got home, Paxton is doing amazing. As a matter of fact, In my eyes he is perfect. He always will be. He is my boy. If you want to get into the technical aspect of his recovery, with all the tests and appointments and therapists, blah, blah, blah, he still is delayed in pretty much everything across the board. He tested low on his speech, physical, and occupational therapy evaluations. And one of tests said he was even bordering on the bottom 2% of his age group. Personally, I could care less what the tests say. However, he is facing a few challenges as he bounces back following his accident. The main issue he is currently faced with is a condition/delay that affects his body awareness, or proprioception. To make a long story short, this affects his brains ability to know the relative position of his body parts in space, and the strength of effort required in a movement. This causes a feeling of physical insecurity. His brain CONSTANTLY needs sensory input to know or sense where his body is in space. It causes him to bounce from one place to another, one item to another, touch, climb, hug, etc so his body is getting enough sensory input. Because of this it's hard for his brain to concentrate on one thing long enough to actually learn to perform that task. He is currently being sent a compression vest that "hugs" him constantly giving his brain that sensory feeling. The other day in therapy they had him wear the vest, and he was able to sit calmly with the therapist and focus on play for 45 min. Which was a big step. Other things that they are focusing on in therapy are his core strength, balance, fine motor control (knowing how to manipulate his hand to perform cognitive tasks), and chewing (he

chomps instead of grinds his food... His dad probably still does that 😜☺). Most of these delays are very subtle, almost to the point that I don't even notice them until they are pointed out. Others are more noticeable. But I feel like he has made tremendous progress in just the short time he has been in therapy. And they anticipate he will be in therapy for 6 months to a year. So by the time he "graduates", he should be as good as new.

Most importantly, his personality remains the same. He may have some exaggerated issues with impulse control here or there, but shoot, what 19 month old doesn't!? But he makes me smile. ALWAYS. His laugh. His smile. The silliness. The craziness!! The feel of his head on my chest when I rock him to bed. And the eager look on his face with his arms raised when I come to get him out of bed in the morning. The sound of all three of my kids playing together. The little things that just make him "Pax". He is truly one of a kind. But as Pax gets better, we all start to heal. Brooklyn is now currently in counseling. That night Brooklyn unfortunately was witness to the whole thing. She saw Pax lying there. And she saw everyone screaming and crying and performing CPR. Everyone tried their best to get her into a different room so she wouldn't have to see but it was too late. Following the accident, Brooklyn experienced nightmares and flashbacks of that night, something I wish my little girl never had to go through. But she has been super strong and is healing and getting better every day. Braelyn met with a counselor as well. Fortunately for her, the counselor concluded she was too young to understand the magnitude of the situation and was going to be (and is) just fine. I've spoken with other family members who have also sought out counseling. And another that mentioned she still cries at random times throughout the day thinking about it. Needless to say It was pretty traumatic for all. Dez and I are doing well. We are both EXTREMELY grateful things turned out the way they did. I think we both try our best to find ways to cope with the whole thing. And Sometimes between that and the crazy schedules of Doctors appointments, work, the kids school and now soccer, things can sometimes be stressful. But it is a learning process and a journey we take together, and I am blessed to have my wife by my side.

We also have a whole new outlook on life. I've learned to NEVER take a second of the time I have with my kids for granted. I am a much more patient father now. And I appreciate every ounce of uniqueness each one of my kids possess. I'm able to stop and take a second to enjoy the little things. And to take pictures. LOTS OF PICTURES. Lol. We haven't missed a day of church since being discharged from the hospital. Brooklyn has developed a very strong faith in God, and we read the children's bible every night before bed. Dez and the girls volunteered at "Feed my Starving Children", preparing food for children in other counties that do not have food to eat. My mother has signed up to volunteer at Phoenix Children's Hospital over the winter as well.

Anyway, I'll wrap this incredibly long rambling up with this. If someone asked me if we are all better after the accident, I would say "no". We still have a lot of healing to do. And a lot of things to figure out. But It really makes you reflect on your life. What's important. What kind of person do you want to be. And what do you want to raise your kids to grow up to be like. Faith.... That maybe things do happen for a reason, and it's all part of Gods master plan. I know for a fact that by the events that unfolded that night, and everything that followed, relationships were mended, friendships were formed, faith was derived and lives reevaluated. And it makes me believe that the positives that came out of the experience were all part of how it was supposed to end. Maybe that's just my way of coping. Maybe that's my way of wrapping my brain around such a traumatic event. Maybe not. But at the least it has made me cherish every second I have with my little boy. And girls. And wife. My family. And my friends. This is my aftermath.

❤□□

Like • Comment • Share • 58 Katie Gibson Riggs, Kim Planks and 55 others13 Comments 4 shares • Comments

Brenda M.: Tears streaming down my face...beautiful, friend, just BEAUTIFUL!!!
Like • Reply • 1 • August 23 at 10:21pm

Robert W.: Bro, why you gotta make me cry? Great update tonight man. You're blessed beyond measure, but I know that you know that.
Like • Reply • 1 • August 23 at 10:44pm

Rach S.: Wow that was a great post. Thank you so much for sharing. I know you all are busy, but we def got to get together soon. Love your family. If you guys need anything let us know;). Hugs to you all
Like • Reply • 1 • August 23 at 10:55pm

Meagan S.: Best thing you've ever written - and I should know. ;) I am so glad to read this. I've been thinking of you all. With your strength and determination and love, you will all emerge stronger than ever. You are already on that path. Family, friends and love. All anyone needs. Keep us updated every now and then. Love to you and your family, Steve. I'll be keeping you in my heart.
Like • Reply • 2 • August 23 at 11:14pm

Desiree M.: I truly believe life is school and everything has a purpose and lesson no matter how difficult. We have a choice to learn or not learn and just play victim. You have taken something awful and very quickly realized the value in it and this is what it's all about. It will take time to heal for sure ! Be the ⍰ that your family needs to get past all this, I think you are doing a wonderful job ! I highly recommend the book Into The Light by john lerma to help reassure you about this experience
https://www.amazon.com/gp/aw/d/1564149722/ref=mp_s_a_1_2
...
Into the Light: Real Life Stories About Angelic Visits, Visions of the Afterlife, and...
amazon.com
Like • Reply • 1 • August 23 at 11:31pm

Ana G.: I'm so happy to know that Paxton is doing great and everything is a healing process as a family!!It was great having you back at work Monday Steven!!And you know your DaVita Family

will always be there for you & your family!!#Davitastrong ❤❤❤
❤❤
Like • Reply • 1 • August 24 at 4:58am • Edited

Brad J.: Your outlook and attitude are commendable beyond compare. As always, wishing you all the very best. Thanks for the updates.
Like • Reply • 1 • August 24 at 8:00am

Cassie M.: There isn't a day that goes by that I don't think about your family. I love the updates and I believe sharing your story has touched us all and made us all have a new outlook on life. Please stop by and visit us from time to time, I would sure love to visit with you guys ❤
Like • Reply • 1 • August 24 at 1:28pm

Dennis S.: Well, I'm just going to have to hijack your post and make this all about me - what about MY anxiety and emotions? I mean, I was at work when you got that horrible phone call and listening to you completely losing it was hard on me, too. I've had to start taking lots and lots of pills for anxiety and depression (and some just to be high) ever since. Oh wait - I was already taking those before that. Okay, but I've been a stressed out basket case since...no wait...I was already like that, too. Of course I'm just totally kidding and trying to make you laugh. Sometimes laughing is just as important in healing as crying. I'm so happy Steve, for you and Dez, so very grateful things turned out as they did, you're all still together as a family and in time everything will reach a new normality and this will all just be an awful memory - but one that you can always be happy with it's outcome. It's brought your entire family together more than ever - and that includes your Davita family as well, you know we'll always be around for support, too. <3
Like • Reply • 2 • August 24 at 4:32pm

Ana G.: replied • 1 Reply

Jeff R.: I wonder if an under armour compression shirt would give the same kind of "hug" feedback?
Like • Reply • August 24 at 8:16pm

Liz G.: Beautiful Steve! I think about your family every day. So much love to you guys! ❤☐ ❤☐
Like • Reply • 1 • August 25 at 12:05am

Nancy B.: Steve I don't think I've ever read anything so beautifully written and so heart felt and honest. I've read it twice and cried twice. So anxious to see all of you in September when I do the road trip with your mother. Take care♥☐.
Like • Reply • 1 • August 25 at 7:20pm

Julie R.: Wow -- no one could have written a better update / summary... and message for all of us. You are an amazing dad with an incredible family. God Bless You ALL.
Like • Reply • 1 • August 25 at 10:33pm

Made in the USA
San Bernardino, CA
06 December 2016